The Civilian Conservation Corps in Wisconsin

THE CIVILIAN CONSERVATION CORPS IN WISCONSIN

Nature's Army at Work

JERRY APPS

WISCONSIN HISTORICAL SOCIETY PRESS

Published by the Wisconsin Historical Society Press
Publishers since 1855

The Wisconsin Historical Society helps people connect to the past by collecting, preserving, and sharing stories. Founded in 1846, the Society is one of the nation's finest historical institutions.
Join the Wisconsin Historical Society: wisconsinhistory.org/membership

Publication of this book was made possible in part by a grant from the Alice E. Smith fellowship fund.

Printed in Canada

Cover design by Andrew J. Brozyna, AJB Design
Typesetting by S4Carlisle Publishing Services

23 22 21   2 3 4 5

Library of Congress Cataloging-in-Publication Data
Names: Apps, Jerold W., 1934– author.
Title: The Civilian Conservation Corps in Wisconsin : nature's army at work / Jerry Apps.
Description: [Madison, Wis.] : Wisconsin Historical Society Press, [2019] | Includes
    bibliographical references and index. |
Identifiers: LCCN 2018034905 (print) | LCCN 2018041065 (e-book) |
    ISBN 9780870209055 (e-book) | ISBN 9780870209048 (pbk. : alk. paper)
Subjects: LCSH: Civilian Conservation Corps (U.S.)—History. | Conservation projects
    (Natural resources)—Wisconsin—History.
Classification: LCC S932.W6 (e-book) | LCC S932.W6 A67 2019 (print) |
    DDC 333.709775—dc23
LC record available at https://lccn.loc.gov/2018034905

*To the CCC boys who saved themselves as they saved
the nation's natural resources.*

CONTENTS

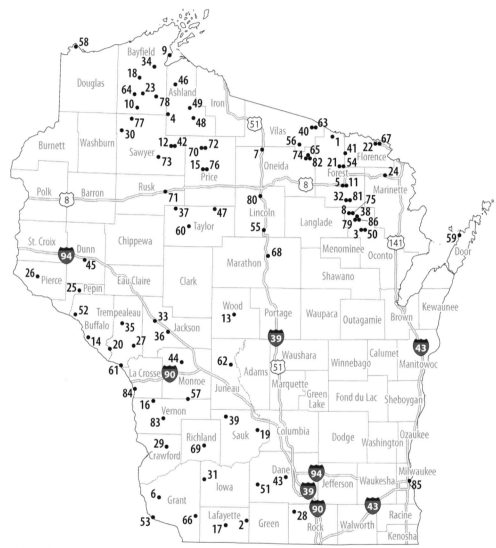

58

Bayfield 9
34
18
Douglas 64 23 46
10 78 Ashland 49 Iron
4 48
77
30 51 Vilas 40 63
12 42 72 56 1 41 22 67
Sawyer 70 7 65 74 54 Florence
73 15 76 82 21 24
Price Oneida 5 11 Forest
Rusk 8 Marinette
Polk 8 Barron 71 32 81 75
37 47 80 8 38
60 Taylor Lincoln 55 Langlade 79 86
St. Croix Chippewa 3 50 141 59
94 Dunn 68 Menominee Oconto Door
26 45 Marathon Shawano
Pierce Eau Claire Clark
25 Pepin
52 Trempealeau 33 Wood Portage Waupaca Outagamie Brown Kewaunee
Buffalo 35 13 Calumet 43
14 20 27 36 Jackson 44 Waushara Winnebago Manitowoc
61 62 51
La Crosse 90 Monroe Adams Marquette Fond du Lac Sheboygan
84 57 Juneau Green Lake
16 Vernon 39 Columbia Dodge Washington Ozaukee
83 19 Sauk
29 Richland Dane Milwaukee
Crawford 69 94 Jefferson Waukesha 85
31 Iowa 43 39 39 90 43 Racine
6 Grant 51 90 Walworth
53 66 Lafayette 28 Rock Kenosha
17 2 Green

MAPPING SPECIALISTS, LTD., FITCHBURG, WI

Approximate Location of CCC Camps in Wisconsin

1. Camp Alvin, Alvin, WI
2. Camp Argyle, Argyle, WI
3. Camp Bear Paw, Mountain, WI
4. Camp Beaver, Clam Lake, WI
5. Camp Blackwell, Laona, WI
6. Camp Bloomington, Bloomington, WI
7. Camp Blue Lake, Minocqua, WI
8. Camp Boot Lake, Townsend, WI
9. Camp Brinks, Washburn, WI
10. Camp Cable, Cable, WI
11. Camp Cavour, Laona, WI
12. Camp Chippewa River, Loretta, WI
13. Camp City Point, Wood County, WI
14. Camp Cochrane, Cochrane, WI
15. Camp Connors Lake, Phillips, WI
16. Camp Coon Valley, Coon Valley, WI
17. Camp Darlington, Darlington, WI
18. Camp Delta, Delta, WI
19. Camp Devil's Lake, Baraboo, WI
20. Camp Dodge, Dodge, WI
21. Camp Double Bend, Newald, WI
22. Camp Dream, Florence, WI
23. Camp Drummond, Drummond, WI
24. Camp Dunbar, Dunbar, WI
25. Camp Durand, Durand, WI
26. Camp Ellsworth, Ellsworth, WI
27. Camp Ettrick, Ettrick, WI
28. Camp Evansville, Evansville, WI
29. Camp Gays Mills, Gays Mills, WI
30. Camp Ghost Creek, Hayward, WI
31. Camp Highland, Highland, WI
32. Camp Himley Lake, Wabeno, WI
33. Camp Hixton, Hixton, WI
34. Camp Horseshoe, Moquah, WI
35. Camp Independence, Independence, WI
36. Camp Irving, Black River Falls, WI
37. Camp Jump River, Jump River, WI
38. Camp Lakewood, Lakewood, WI
39. Camp LaValle, LaValle, WI
40. Camp Lily Pad, Phelps, WI
41. Camp Long Lake, Long Lake, WI
42. Camp Loretta, Loretta, WI

43. Camp Madison, Madison, WI
44. Camp McCoy, between Sparta and Tomah, WI
45. Camp Menomonie, Menomonie, WI
46. Camp Mineral Lake, Marengo, WI
47. Camp Mondeaux River, Westboro, WI
48. Camp Moose River, Glidden, WI
49. Camp Morse, Morse, WI
50. Camp Mountain, Mountain, WI
51. Camp Mount Horeb, Mount Horeb, WI
52. Camp Nelson, Nelson, WI
53. Camp Nelson Dewey, Cassville, WI
54. Camp Newald, Newald, WI
55. Camp New Wood, Merrill, WI
56. Camp Nine Mile, Eagle River, WI
57. Camp Ontario, Ontario, WI
58. Camp Pattison, Superior, WI
59. Camp Peninsular, Fish Creek, WI
60. Camp Perkinstown, Perkinstown, WI
61. Camp Perrot, Trempealeau, WI
62. Camp Petenwell, Necedah, WI
63. Camp Phelps, Phelps, WI
64. Camp Pigeon Lake, Drummond, WI
65. Camp Pine River, Three Lakes, WI
66. Camp Platteville, Platteville, WI
67. Camp Rainbow, Florence, WI
68. Camp Rib Mountain, Wausau, WI
69. Camp Richland Center, Richland Center, WI
70. Camp Riley Creek, Fifield, WI
71. Camp Rusk, Glen Flora, WI
72. Camp Sailor Lake, Fifield, WI
73. Camp Sawyer, Winter, WI
74. Camp Scott Lake, Three Lakes, WI
75. Camp Section Eleven, Townsend, WI
76. Camp Sheep Ranch, Phillips, WI
77. Camp Smith Lake, Seeley, WI
78. Camp Taylor Lake, Grandview, WI
79. Camp Thunder River, Lakewood, WI
80. Camp Tomahawk, Tomahawk, WI
81. Camp Trump Lake, Wabeno, WI
82. Camp Virgin Lake, Three Lakes, WI
83. Camp Viroqua, Viroqua, WI
84. Camp West Salem, La Crosse, WI
85. Camp Whitnall, Milwaukee, WI
86. Camp Wolf River, Lakewood, WI

PREFACE

I'm regularly asked, "Where do you get the ideas for your books?" The answer is both simple and complicated. Often times, when I am chopping wood, or working in to my garden, or merely hiking in my woodlot, an idea for a book will pop into my head, coming from I know not where. When I am on the road, speaking at local historical societies, libraries, bookstores, and farmers' groups, someone will take me aside and say, "Have you thought about doing a book on . . . ?" The topics range all the way from outhouses (no book coming on these less-than-fondly remembered structures) to my memories of water and its importance in society.

Topping the list of ideas for new books are those that come from booksellers. Booksellers know what their customers want, and I listen to them when they make suggestions. That is exactly what happened with the idea for this book. I was attending the Heartland Fall Forum—a gathering of booksellers, publishers, and authors alternatively held in Minneapolis and Chicago—in 2014 in Minneapolis. There I chatted a bit with Jane Janke, from Janke Book Store in Wausau, Wisconsin. I've known Jane for many years, have signed books at her bookstore, and value her judgment about what customers are interested in these days.

"Have you thought about doing a book on the CCC in Wisconsin?" Jane asked.

"Well, no," I honestly replied.

"Well, you should think about it," Jane said. Jane knew I had written essentially nothing about the logging industry and related topics. I knew that the CCC, or the Civilian Conservation Corps, was heavily involved in helping reforest the great cutover region of northern Wisconsin and was active in the development of both state and national parks. But somehow I had overlooked writing anything specific about the CCC.

I said I'd think about it. For every book idea, I first consider if it fits my writing niche—the rural Midwest, small towns, rural communities, farmers, and environmental concerns. Then I ask, "What do I already know about this topic?" I knew about the CCC when I was a kid—it began the year before I was born, and by the time I began school in 1939, the organization was going strong. Someone had told me that the CCC helped construct the fishponds and other structures at the Wild Rose Fish Hatchery, a place where we often took visitors who came to our farm. I also remember when a crew of CCC boys came to our farm—it must have been in the late 1930s— and asked if they could go through our woodlot in search of the currant and gooseberry shrubs that host the white pine blister rust that was killing many white pines in Wisconsin and elsewhere.

Years later, when I was teaching at the School of the Arts in Rhinelander, I visited the CCC museum located in that city and learned about life in a CCC camp, the kind of work the young men did, the tools they used, and much more.

Finally, in making a decision about a new book project, I ask, "Is this something that interests me enough that I would spend hundreds of hours researching, writing, and rewriting to create a well-researched and informative piece of writing that is filled with stories and easy to read?"

As I began doing the preliminary research on this topic, I soon became fascinated with how, during the depths of the Great Depression, a program such as the CCC could emerge and provide long-standing benefits to the young men who enrolled in the program as well as profound improvements to the natural environment. I decided that this was a project I must do.

PART I

BACKGROUND

1

INTRODUCTION

They came from farms and cities, from Chicago, Detroit, and Milwaukee, from small towns like Pine River and Tomahawk, Wisconsin, and from productive farms and those that were struggling. They represented a generation of the nation's young men who, through no fault of their own, could not find a job because there were no jobs. Many of these young men were hungry, as were their families. It was a dreary, dangerous time. Nearly two million men had given up any hope of finding work. They traveled on foot and in freight cars. They slept in caves or shantytowns as they drifted aimlessly around the country searching for a job or a bite to eat. Nearly 250,000 of these so-called tramps were young men in their teens and early twenties, "wandering the land looking for a future."[1]

Starting in 1933, many of these forgotten young men signed up for a new government program dedicated to conservation. The program eventually became known as the Civilian Conservation Corps, often shortened to the CCC. The mission of the CCC was simple: put young men to work on the land. People were skeptical, though. It was a new idea for the nation to devote a sizeable amount of money and manpower for the improvement and protection of the nation's natural resources. Another top-down government program, they said. A handout of taxpayer money to the poor, they said. But times were tough, across the country and in Wisconsin. People were willing to try something—anything—because they had to eat and have a roof over their heads. The number of people having neither was on the increase. So the CCC was born out of a clumsy administrative arrangement between four major government agencies: the Departments of Agriculture, Labor, and the Interior—and, of all organizations, the War Department. On paper it looked

3

impossible. What connection could there be among the War Department, the Department of Agriculture, the Department of Labor, and the Department of the Interior? Their missions are undeniably different. The army fights wars and defends us from wars. The Department of Agriculture is about food production, saving soil, and managing forests. The Department of Labor is responsible for overseeing standards of employment in the United States. And the Department of the Interior, among other duties, manages our national parks. But the agencies came together. They cooperated, and the program worked—beyond anything anyone could have imagined.

That's not to say that the CCC didn't have its critics. Some wondered if those who organized the program saw the irony of having a program run by the military be given a civilian name. But the accomplishments of the CCC soon overshadowed concerns about it. Young men had work that benefited themselves and their families. Enrollees received thirty dollars a month, twenty-five dollars of which went home to help impoverished families afford food and shelter.

Enrollees were often given patches like this one to wear or keep as souvenirs. COURTESY OF JAMES SKARDA

Recruits decorated their bunks and barracks with pennants and other CCC paraphernalia. COURTESY OF STEVE APPS. PHOTO USED WITH PERMISSION FROM THE PIONEER PARK HISTORICAL COMPLEX

For the young men who worked for the CCC, the benefit turned out to be much greater than a job and a monthly salary. Many expressed some version of this sentiment: "We came to the CCC as boys and we left as men." Young men learned how to work, gained employment skills, and some even learned to read and write. They learned about discipline and following orders. They developed leadership skills. And they learned how to get along with one another—a necessity when living two-hundred-plus men to a camp and forty or more men to a single bunkhouse.

While these boys were becoming men, they were making a tremendous contribution to the improvement of the natural resources of the United States—something that had been ignored for several generations. The CCC arguably changed the attitudes of millions of Americans who had believed that the country's abundant natural resources were there for the taking and could never be depleted or despoiled. By planting trees and building windbreaks, introducing contour farming and erosion control, and developing state and national parks, these young men made Americans see how terrible conditions in the environment had become by the early 1930s. Forest depletion, soil erosion, and floods had taken their toll on the American landscape—so the CCC did something about it. They went to work.

2

THE GREAT DEPRESSION AND NATURAL RESOURCES ABUSE

When World War I ended with the Armistice taking place on the eleventh hour of the eleventh day of the eleventh month of 1918, citizens of the United States believed their soldiers had fought in and won the war to end all wars.

After the Armistice, better times came quickly to America. By the early 1920s, with memories of World War I and its devastation beginning to fade, Americans began making money, kicking up their heels, and having a good time. During the Roaring Twenties, there was indeed much to get excited about. People were on the move and altering the look of the American landscape like never before. The US Census taken in 1920 revealed that for the first time, the nation's urban population exceeded the number of rural residents. Farmers, long seen as the backbone of the nation, were increasingly considered "hicks" and "hayseeds" by urbanites embracing a new era of fads and change. It was a time to enjoy life at its fullest, for women as well as men.[1] When Congress ratified the Nineteenth Amendment to the US Constitution in 1920, women gained the right to vote. With it, an emboldened new kind of woman emerged on the scene. This new woman openly smoked, drank, danced, and wore her hair short. These societal rule-breakers became known as flappers.[2]

Change came at a rapid pace. On November 2, 1920, KDKA in Pittsburgh, Pennsylvania, became the first commercial radio station in the nation to regularly broadcast programs. In 1923, U.S. Steel implemented the eight-hour workday. Charles Lindbergh flew the *Spirit of St. Louis* from New York to Paris in thirty-three and a half hours in 1927 and immediately became a national hero. The first talking movie was shown that same year. It featured Al Jolson and marked the beginning of the end for the era of silent film. In 1927, Babe Ruth hit sixty home runs for the New York Yankees, and, in 1928, Walt Disney introduced Mickey Mouse to the world. Henry Ford brought out the Model A in 1927, a successor to the popular Model T. By the end of the decade, Ford had sold 1.5 million Model A cars. Indeed, the automobile was becoming such a fixture of American life that Herbert Hoover, the Republican nominee for president in 1928, campaigned on the promise of "A chicken in every pot, a car in every garage."[3] Hoover defeated Al Smith in the election. With new inventions, new innovations, new leadership, and old morality rules falling by the wayside, the good times rolled. Optimistic Americans believed in a bright future of greater good fortune and bold innovation.

But there were serious downsides in the 1920s as well. The Eighteenth Amendment to the US Constitution, which prohibited the manufacture and sale of alcoholic beverages in the United States, became the law of the land in 1920. The new law, though, did not prevent the consumption of alcohol. Far from it. Speakeasies were everywhere. Organized crime, with its bootleggers, killings, and crime rampages, made a mockery of prohibition and the temperance movement. Al Capone became a name everyone knew. His gang of bootleggers made sure speakeasies had sufficient booze for the ever-thirsty patrons who crowded through their doors. Chicago became known as a lawless city in large part because the law did little to stop enterprising men like Capone and his gangsters.

By the end of the decade, the good times that many Americans believed would last forever were the stuff of memory. On September 2, 1929, the Dow Jones Industrial Average reached an all-time high of 381.2 points. Weeks later, on October 24, or Black Thursday, traders sold thirteen million shares. The selling spree continued five days later, when panicked investors sold sixteen million shares on Black Tuesday. By November 13, 1929, the Dow had plummeted to 199 points. The market had lost thirty billion dollars in devalued stocks. The banks panicked. An economic collapse, the Great Depression, had begun.

The Great Depression would last until 1939. It brought on a decade of unemployment, hunger, desperation, and agony. It was the worst economic calamity in US history—no one saw it coming, and no one knew what to do about it.

TEENAGE HOBOS

Jim Mitchell ran away from his Kenosha, Wisconsin, home in 1933, when he was seventeen years old. He remembered when his dad came home from work and declared that he had lost his job. His father began to cry. Jim recalled that the family lived off their relatives, eating at his grandmother's house. Jim decided it was time to lighten the load on his family, and he ran away. During the depths of the Depression, more than 250,000 teenagers roamed America—some because they felt they were a burden on their family but most because no jobs were available.

Mitchell and a friend, Peter Lijinski, hopped freight trains across the Midwest. He remembered, "You went on the road and you exchanged one misery for another. You were always filthy and constantly hungry. You'd take whatever odd jobs you could. We did everything from mowing lawns to cleaning grease traps in restaurants. It was humiliating, but sometimes you panhandled. Nothing was happening and there was no direction in your life."[4]

Mitchell and his friend met an army officer after they had gotten work at a carnival. The army officer suggested they might do better by joining the Civilian Conservation Corps. The two young men became enrollees at Camp New Wood, located nine miles north of Merrill, Wisconsin.

Mitchell discovered a great diversity of boys in the CCC. He remembered, "We lived forty men to a barrack; two bunks down there would be a farm kid who couldn't read or write. If he got a letter from home, somebody read it to him. You could go up a couple more bunks and find a medical student who dropped out of the University of Wisconsin. Another boy's father had an automobile dealership that went bust. Some kids were hoods from the cities." But for all of these boys, no matter their circumstances, Mitchell summed up their CCC experience with the words "Thank God, somebody cares about me."[5]

Wisconsin and the Depression

The Great Depression hit Wisconsin hard, especially in Milwaukee. By the 1920s, the city had become a major industrial center. Milwaukee beer barons, who at one time led the world in beer production, were still smarting from prohibition, which forced them to close their breweries. From 1929 to 1933, the number of jobs available in Milwaukee fell 75 percent. Twenty percent of Milwaukee's citizens received some form of direct relief from Milwaukee County.

To add to the woes of the economic collapse, a severe drought in the Midwest and Southwest destroyed crops and uprooted people. Dust storms clouded the sky day after dreadful day, with the sun hidden as if it were night. Those living in "the Dust Bowl," the name given to a great swath of land in the Oklahoma and Texas panhandles, as well as areas of Kansas, Colorado, and New Mexico, watched the wind blow their land to dust and their livelihoods into the wind. The land that had once sustained industrious farmers and a thriving economy had become inhospitable and unforgiving. By 1940, more than 2.5 million people had left the Dust Bowl region in search of a better life elsewhere.[6]

Wisconsin farmers, especially those working sandy soils, got a taste of Wisconsin's own dust bowl that tore up crops and depleted soil. Farmers who had substantial mortgages on their farms lost them when they were not able to make the monthly payments. They joined the city unemployed searching for a way to survive the catastrophe that had visited the state and the nation. Most Wisconsin farmers were somewhat less likely to suffer from lack of food or shelter than those living in urban areas, but farmers saw agricultural prices and their property values plummet.

In 1929, 47 percent of Wisconsin's population of nearly three million lived on farms. The Depression's impact on Wisconsin's rural population was especially severe. Some regions suffered more than others. A 1936 survey revealed some interesting variation in what the authors of the study called the "relative financial condition of counties." Researchers looked at such factors as tax levy delinquency, extent of state aid per teacher, amount of gross farm income, percentage of farm income spent on real estate taxes, per capita wealth based on assessed value of property, and relief situation. The study focused on rural Wisconsin and discovered, not surprisingly, that southeastern Wisconsin counties fared best and counties in the north fared worst. The researchers ranked the relative financial conditions of the state from best to worst as follows: southeastern, southwestern, central, north central, and northern regions. The cutover region, comprising as many as twenty counties in the north, had the poorest financial condition characterized by low gross farm income, high tax delinquency, and a heavy relief burden (welfare payments).[7]

Many of Wisconsin's small banks closed as one of the immediate outcomes of the Depression. Some people lost all their savings. The Wisconsin legislature, recognizing the severity of job loss in the state, passed America's first unemployment compensation law in early 1932, which became a model for the country to follow. But the law provided little immediate help to those who needed it, as the state, like the nation, was overwhelmed with unemployment. In 1933, the Bureau of Labor Statistics estimated that nearly thirteen million Americans were out of work, or about one-fourth of the labor force. In March of that year, the number of unemployed workers in the United States reached 15.5 million.[8]

People in a Green Bay employment office look for work during the Great Depression.
WHI IMAGE ID 24514

Desperate people began to take desperate measures to meet the Depression's challenges and solve its problems. Communists on the left and fascists on the right thought they had the solution to the nation's economic woes. Milwaukee saw labor strikes increase sevenfold from 1933 to 1934. Workers in industry hoping to keep their jobs and prevent falling wages put their faith in union leaders whose job it was to influence industry management and policymakers. The Wisconsin legislature passed a comprehensive labor code in 1931, giving workers the right to organize and participate in union activities. But this legislation, too, offered little immediate aid. How could it? The effects of the US economic collapse spread quickly around the globe, hitting Europe especially hard. Thus, few people anywhere had money to buy much of anything. Without a market for products, there were few jobs.[9]

Something needed to be done. But what? And by whom?

NATURAL RESOURCES ABUSE

Wisconsin has always had an abundance of natural resources: thousands of lakes and rivers, rich agricultural soils, several million acres of forest land, shoreline on Lakes Superior and Michigan, fish and wildlife to satisfy the sportsman, and birds and wildflowers and natural beauty for everyone to enjoy. But humans are prone to take for granted natural resources and abuse them.

In the late 1860s, logging became one of Wisconsin's major economic activities. By 1893, logging had reached its peak, and Wisconsin had become a world leader in the lumber industry, producing some 3.5 billion board feet annually. Sawmills sprung up on Wisconsin's rivers and streams. Waterways were dammed to create power for the mills. By 1898, loggers had harvested eight million acres of Wisconsin's forest land, creating a vast area that became known as the "cutover." In the same year, the federal government conducted a survey of Wisconsin's northern forestlands. B. F. Fernow, author of the report, wrote, "In almost every town in this region logging has been carried [out] on eight million of the seventeen million acres of forest, which are now 'cut over' lands largely burned over and waste brush lands, and one-half of it as nearly desert as it can become in the climate of Wisconsin."[10]

Huge numbers of logs were harvested from the forests of northern Wisconsin during the late nineteenth and early twentieth centuries. WHI IMAGE ID 82796

By the early 1930s, the vast majority of the valuable timber in northern Wisconsin had been removed or destroyed by fire. Harvesting occurred in two major waves. First, the pines were cut and floated down rivers to sawmills. Next, when railroads came into the north, loggers cut the hardwoods, maple primarily, and shipped the logs out of the region by rail. Generally, loggers took the larger, more valuable trees, leaving behind smaller and often less desirable species such as birch and aspen. By 1936, what remained in the once great forests of the north was slash (brush and limbs) left over from the harvest, along with young second-growth timber of less desirable tree species. Moreover, the entire area was plagued by forest fires that roared through the region, destroying what remained on the forestland. In 1933, drought and forest fires ravaged thousands of acres in northern Wisconsin. In Lincoln County, for example, records show that more than fifty thousand acres of land was burned over. During a dust storm, nineteen thousand acres went up in flames because fire wardens

Logging produced a barren "cutover" region in northern Wisconsin. The tree harvest left the land vulnerable to soil erosion. WHI IMAGE ID 3991

Stumps were removed from the cutover region to make the land arable. WHI IMAGE ID 92803

and fire spotters, even from their towers, could not see through the clouds of dust sweeping across the sky.[11]

When land had been cleared of its valuable timber, lumber companies sold their denuded forest acres to land speculators. Speculators, in turn, parceled out their purchases and sold smaller tracts of land to would-be farmers. Many of these aspiring farmers were immigrants. New farmers removed stumps, planted crops, and struggled to earn a living on land that eventually proved to be more suitable for trees than farm crops.[12]

In their efforts to make a better life for themselves, settlers, usually unknowingly, contributed to the environmental destruction of northern Wisconsin. When they straightened out trout streams so water would run off their fields more quickly, settlers did terrible damage to the fish habitat. As one writer put it, the farmers "cut away the cover from the streams; the fish died out. Streams dried up; lake levels dropped; fire turned the green woods black."[13] In the marshy areas of the state in central and southeastern Wisconsin, ditch diggers drained marshes to open more land for farming. The state legislature aided this effort by providing legislation to legally establish drainage districts and by encouraging farmers to work these former wetlands.[14] This, too, did more harm than good. Farmers, accustomed to plowing up and down hills in the hilly regions of the state, contributed to soil erosion as rains washed away topsoil, created gullies, and slowly destroyed the land. And on the sandy flatlands of central Wisconsin, farmers plowed vast fields and planted them to crops, such as potatoes, corn, and wheat. Just as the land had been blown away in the Dust Bowl region, so too did the land suffer when drought came to the Midwest.[15]

Such was the calamitous economic and environmental situation in Wisconsin when Franklin Delano Roosevelt and Herbert Hoover sought election to the presidency of the United States in 1932.

3

CCC LEGISLATION AND ADMINISTRATIVE ORGANIZATION

The United States was in dire straits during the presidential election of 1932. The country was suffering from the worst economic depression it had ever known. As one writer noted, "The 1932 Presidential election was more a cry for help than it was an election."[1] Thousands of unemployed Americans roamed the cities and countryside, looking for work. In Wisconsin, "people turned from sneaking bootleg beer into jazz halls to devising ways of surviving the worst depression in the nation's history."[2]

Franklin Delano Roosevelt, a gentleman farmer with a great love for his Hyde Park estate in New York, had long been interested in conservation. The idea of employing young men to work on conservation projects had been used by the Forest Service in California and the state of Washington at the beginning of the Great Depression. Also, Denmark, Norway, Bulgaria, Austria, and the Netherlands had developed similar work programs for the unemployed. The Weimar Republic in Germany created a young worker program to combat unemployment in Germany's major cities. Invigorated by Adolf Hitler and his Nazi Party, it became an important part of the Nazi propaganda machine and was considered the most controversial job program in the world.[3]

Roosevelt was aware of what was going on in California, Washington, and Europe. When he was governor of New York, he created conservation jobs with the New York Temporary Emergency Relief Administration.[4] When Roosevelt accepted the Democratic presidential nomination on

July 1, 1932, he began talking about the need to fight soil erosion and enhance the country's timber resources by putting unemployed young men to work, especially those from large urban areas.

On November 8, 1932, Roosevelt won the presidency in a landslide victory over Herbert Hoover. Republicans suffered losses in the House of Representatives and the Senate as well, where Democrats won majorities. During his inauguration speech on March 4, 1933, Roosevelt promised to immediately put into action the "New Deal" proposals he had campaigned on.[5] True to his promise, Roosevelt wasted no time. He spent his first one hundred days as president making his New Deal a reality. On March 9, 1933, he called Congress into emergency session and proposed a program "to recruit thousands of unemployed young men, enroll them in a peacetime army, and send them into battle against destruction and erosion of our natural resources."[6] The program was called the Emergency Conservation Work program; it would later be officially known as the

EXCERPTS FROM THE UNEMPLOYMENT RELIEF ACT OF MARCH 31, 1933 (SEVENTY-THIRD CONGRESS, S. 598)

The following passages appeared in the Unemployment Relief Act of March 31, 1933. They outline the need for and purpose of the Emergency Conservation Work program, which would eventually be called the Civilian Conservation Corps.

An Act for the relief of unemployment through the performance of useful public work, and for other purposes.

Be it enacted by the Senate and House of Representatives of the United States of America in Congress assembled, That for the purpose of relieving the acute condition of widespread distress and unemployment now existing in the United States, and in order to provide for the restoration of the country's depleted natural resources and the advancement of an orderly program of useful public works, the President is authorized, under such rules and regulations as he may prescribe and by utilizing such existing departments or agencies he

Civilian Conservation Corps. President Roosevelt signed the legislation on March 31, 1933.

The CCC had its critics from the start. Some of the initial resistance came from union leaders, who saw the program's potential to recruit nonunion members. Organized labor also opposed the CCC because it believed that the "involvement of the Army . . . might lead to regimentation of labor."[7] Labor's concerns, however, were scarcely prohibiting. The country, ever deeper in recession, was ready to accept any reasonable idea to help remedy the effects of the Depression. Undeterred, President Roosevelt marched forward with his plans and promised to place 250,000 young men in the CCC by the end of July.[8]

Roosevelt's plan was so audacious and ambitious that no one thought the new president could keep his promise. It was a short time until July, and several important hurdles had to be cleared before the first camp could open. But it happened—at a pace unprecedented in American history. Indeed, as one writer marveled, "The speed with which the plan moved

may designate, to provide for employing citizens of the United States or to the several States which are suitable for timber production, the prevention of forest fires, floods and soil erosion, plant pest and disease control, construction, maintenance or repair of paths, trails, and fire lanes in the national parks and national forests, and other work on the public domain, national and State, and Government reservations incidental to or necessary in connection with any projects of the character enumerated, as the President may determine to be desirable. . . .

The President is further authorized by regulation, to provide for housing the persons so employed and for furnishing them with such subsistence, clothing, medical attendance and hospitalization, and cash allowance, as may be necessary, during the period they are so employed, and, in his discretion, to provide for the transportation of such persons to and from the places of employment. That in employing citizens for the purposes of this Act no discrimination shall be made on account of race, color, or creed; and no person under conviction for serving sentence therefor shall be employed under provisions of the Act.[9]

through proposal, authorization, implementation and operation was a miracle of cooperation among all branches and agencies of the federal government. It was a mobilization of men, material and transportation on a scale never before known in time of peace."[10]

From FDR's inauguration on March 4, 1933, to the induction of the first CCC enrollee on April 7, only thirty-four days elapsed. In between, Senate Bill S. 598 was introduced on March 27. The bill passed both houses of Congress and was on the president's desk for signature on March 31. Executive Order 6101, dated April 5, 1933, authorized the creation of the CCC and the appointment of its director. It also established an advisory council that included the secretaries of war, labor, agriculture, and the interior.[11] The executive order also called for the transfer of ten million dollars to the CCC from "unobligated balances of the appropriation for the emergency construction of public buildings contained in the Act approved on July 21, 1932."[12]

EXECUTIVE ORDER 6101, APRIL 5, 1933

These excerpts are taken from Executive Order 6101, dated April 5, 1933. In them, President Roosevelt authorizes and funds the Emergency Conservation Work program, names its first director, and appoints its advisory council.

> By virtue of the authority vested in me by the act of Congress entitled "An Act for the relief of unemployment through the performance of useful public work, and for other purposes," approved March 31, 1933 (Public No. 5, 73d Congress), it is hereby ordered that:
>
> 1. For the purpose of carrying out the provisions of said Act, Robert Fechner is hereby appointed Director of Emergency Conservation Work at an annual rate of compensation of $12,000, less the reduction prescribed in subparagraph (b), Section 2, Title II, of the Act of Congress entitled "An Act to maintain the credit of the United States Government" (Public No. 2, 73d Congress), approved March 20, 1933.

To run the new organization, Roosevelt tapped Robert Fechner, vice president of the American Federation of Labor. Naming Fechner director was a strategic move done to put down organized labor's worries.[13]

Once the Department of Labor received its mandate for participation in the CCC, W. Frank Persons, the Labor Department's official representative, immediately invited representatives from seventeen of the nation's largest cities to Washington, DC, to discuss plans and policies for selecting CCC applicants. There was no time to establish a new nationwide organization to select participants, so existing state employment relief agencies were asked to assume the responsibility. Procedures for selection would come from Fechner's office. The guidelines for prospective enrollees were:

- Men eighteen to twenty-five years of age

- Physically fit and unmarried

2. The Secretary of War, the Secretary of Agriculture, the Secretary of the Interior, and the Secretary of Labor each shall appoint a representative, and said representatives shall constitute an Advisory Council to the Director of Emergency Conservation Work.

3. There is hereby established in the Treasury a fund of $10,000,000 by the transfer of an equal amount from the unobligated balances of the appropriation for emergency construction of public buildings contained in the act approved July 21, 1932, as authorized by Section 4 of said Act of March 31, 1933, which fund shall be subject to requisition by the said Robert Fechner, as Director Emergency Conservation Work, and the departments and establishments furnishing such supplies and materials shall be reimbursed therefor in accordance with instructions of the President.

4. Reimbursement, if any, to the departments or establishments for other services rendered shall be made in accordance with instructions of the President.[14]

- Unemployed

- Citizens of the United States

- The names of eligible men should be selected first from the lists of families receiving public aid.

- Young men selected "were to be young men of character, clean cut, purposeful and ambitious."[15]

The first CCC man came aboard on April 7, 1933. Ten days later, the first CCC camp opened at Luray, Virginia. Called Camp Roosevelt, the camp was established in the George Washington National Forest. The site was chosen for its strategic proximity to Washington, DC. Curious lawmakers and citizens could easily travel to Camp Roosevelt to catch a glimpse of what the CCC was about and what it could do. In August 1933, with lots

The CCC waged an aggressive public ad campaign to generate support for its mission. Posters like this one were common. WHI IMAGE ID 5762

of publicity, Roosevelt toured the camp to show the country how his New Deal program was working.[16]

By early July 1933, CCC enrollees numbered 250,000 plus another 25,000 war veterans. In addition, some 25,000 local experienced men, or LEM, were employed in 1,463 CCC camps in operation by that time. Young men signed up in droves. For example, on May 15, 1933, 5,890 young men enrolled. The next day another 8,100 signed on for service, followed by 10,500 more on May 17. Enrollment peaked on June 1 when the CCC welcomed 13,843 fresh recruits. By the beginning of June 1933, more than 150,000 young men were waiting for assignment to regular work camps.[17] Later that summer, 12,000 Native Americans were added to the CCC rolls in a special division eventually called the CCC-ID, or the Civilian Conservation Corps-Indian Division. Native Americans worked under the supervision of the Bureau of Indian Affairs and tribal leaders on reservations across the country.[18]

VETERANS ADDED

Officials almost immediately recognized the need to expand enrollment criteria. People took notice of the fact that not only were the nation's young men out of work and living in families that were barely surviving, many World War I and Spanish-American War veterans were also unemployed. To help, Executive Order 6129, dated May 11, 1933, authorized the Veterans Administration to select 25,000 veterans of World War I and previous wars for service in the CCC. The selection process began June 12. Fechner later increased the number of veterans to add to 28,225. By the end of the month, 5,000 more veterans, this time from drought-stricken regions of the country, had joined the ranks of the CCC.

There was a limit to how many veterans each state could send to its CCC camps. Quotas varied and were based on the 1930 census. To be eligible for CCC service, a veteran "must have served with the armed forces of the United States during the World War and/or prior war and have been honorably discharged therefrom, must have been unemployed, and a citizen of the United States."[19] The veterans served in camps with other veterans apart from younger CCC enrollees. Veterans did the same work, however, assigned to others in the CCC. Given the tall logistical hurdles the CCC had to clear during its earliest days, it is perhaps not surprising that the US Army led the way when times were tough. Historian Paul W. Glad points out that "As was the case with many of the New Deal agencies created during the Hundred Days, disorder and confusion at first hampered CCC efforts. The Army quickly moved to exert a controlling influence, however, and within three months' time, the Civilian Conservation Corps developed into the largest peacetime government labor force in American history."[20]

Eventually, early opposition to the massive governmental program evaporated. The CCC had tremendous public support from both Republicans and Democrats. Even Colonel Robert R. McCormick, publisher of the conservative *Chicago Tribune* and a longtime adversary of FDR, supported what the CCC was doing. McCormick had good cause to think as he did, as a Chicago judge said he believed the CCC was responsible for a 55 percent reduction in crime in the Windy City.[21]

By 1934, more than 300,000 members were enrolled nationally in the CCC, including 250,000 regular recruits, 12,000 Native Americans, 28,000 veterans, and 25,000 LEM. In a 1938 report, Fechner wrote about the early accomplishments of CCC enrollees. He claimed that "a remarkable amount of work had been done despite the fact that the majority of the enrollees were inexperienced and great many wholly ignorant of the fundamentals of the work they were doing."[22]

One interesting feature of the CCC's organization is how existing federal agencies were involved and responsible for all aspects of the program. No new agency was created. As director, Fechner was responsible for getting four agencies of the federal government to work together: the Department of Labor, the War Department, the Department of the Interior, and the Department of Agriculture. Representatives from these departments served Fechner in advisory roles and acted as liaison officers directing traffic between the CCC and their respective agencies.

One of Fechner's immediate tasks, with the help of his advisory council, was to make clear which agency was responsible for what. The various departmental responsibilities were defined as noted below.

The Department of Labor
Responsible for the selection of those enrolled in the CCC (except war veterans who were chosen by the Veterans Administration).

The War Department

Responsible for intake of men selected by the Department of Labor and Veterans Administration; providing transportation to enrollees; assigning recruits for physical fitness conditioning; providing discipline, medical care, and housing; and keeping general order and welfare in the camps.

Without the army's experience, resources, and leadership, the CCC would likely never have gotten off the ground. For eight hours a day, five days a week, CCC men were supervised by representatives from the Department of the Interior or the Department of Agriculture. The rest of the time, a CCC man was the responsibility of the army. From April 1933 to July 1933, the army processed 275,000 CCC applicants, organizing them into more than 1,400 companies of two hundred men each—all scattered across the United States and its territories. Camps were set up in every state, as well as in Hawaii, Alaska, Puerto Rico, and the Virgin Islands. Enrollment peaked at the end of 1935, when there were five hundred thousand men located in 2,600 camps. California alone had more than 150 camps. The greatest concentration of CCC personnel was in the Sixth Civilian Conservation Corps District of the First Corps Area, in the Winooski River Valley of Vermont. In December 1933, enlisted personnel and supervisors there totaled more than 5,300 and occupied four large camps.[23]

After representatives from the Department of Labor processed a young man for CCC entry, he immediately came under the watchful care of the army. Upon selection, a CCC recruit was asked to report to an army base. The army administered a physical examination and vaccinations for infectious disease, then transported the recruit to one of fifty army camps around the country, where he went through a physically demanding training regimen. Because many CCC young men were city boys out of work, they were also badly out of shape and in no condition to take on hard labor in the woods and fields—hence the need for several weeks of exercise at an army base.

The army almost immediately faced a transportation challenge. Most men new to the CCC lived in the eastern United States, far from the camps in the Midwest and West. The army quickly mobilized the nation's transportation system to move young men by rail and bus from induction centers to army bases.[24] Once new CCC inductees had finished a few weeks of training, the army put them on trucks, buses, or trains bound for a camp that in some instances was halfway across America.

In addition to preparing young men for various tasks to be completed in camps, the army had the responsibility of planning the layout of the camps, furnishing tents, and providing material for and supervision of camp construction. The army equipped CCC enrollees with a bed and bedding, procured and prepared meals, organized recreational and educational activities, and offered medical and hospital care when needed. Perhaps most important, it was the army that paid each CCC laborer five dollars at the end of the month, sending what remained of his thirty-dollar salary home to his family.

Typically, each camp was assigned two Regular Army officers, one officer from the Officers' Reserve Corps, and four Regular Army enlisted men, usually of higher rank. Officers were not in short supply, as Roosevelt had ordered early graduation of cadets at the service academies. Some Regular Army officers were even withdrawn from regular duty to serve in the CCC.[25] Later, Regular Army officers were replaced with Officers' Reserve Corps officers. The switch was one of the many unforeseen benefits of the CCC. The program offered meaningful employment opportunities to Officers' Reserve Corps officers, affording them the chance to command and lead young men through practical and purposeful situations. Officers did more than their jobs, though, and their importance to the camps cannot be overstated. Army personnel were often father figures to young men in

Some enrollees stayed in tents before barracks and other buildings could be constructed in camp. This photo shows Camp Bloomington when it was still a "tent city." WHI IMAGE ID 54601

need of direction and guidance. Officers were trusted advisers and, when necessary, disciplinarians.[26]

Of course, the younger CCC Officers' Reserve Corps officers had no idea that they were learning lessons that would one day serve them well in combat on the other side of the world. When the United States entered World War II in 1941, thousands of men who had been CCC Officers' Reserve Corps officers signed up to fight and once again serve their country.

The Department of the Interior
Responsible for overseeing CCC jobs related to national and state park development.

The Department of Agriculture
Responsible for leading CCC efforts outside national and state park land. Department of Agriculture staff in the Soil Conservation Service and the Forest Service worked hand in hand with CCC employees to improve soil quality and conservation efforts around the country.

Originally housed in the Department of the Interior, the Soil Erosion Service was organized in 1933. In 1935, it was transferred to the Department of Agriculture and renamed the Soil Conservation Service.[27] Soil conservation technicians supervised CCC efforts to control erosion and practice good soil conservation. The first major coordinated effort to do so took place at Coon Valley in southwestern Wisconsin.

Given that so much of the CCC's work took place in the forested areas of the United States, it is not surprising that the Forest Service played a leading role in supervising CCC projects across America. By June 29, 1933, 529 camps had been approved for forestry work. Of the CCC camps organized during its first year of operation, about half of them involved forestry projects.[28]

From the beginning, Forest Service officials had to take a different approach to their new labor force. Many Forest Service professionals were accustomed to giving orders to and taking orders from men who knew what they were doing in the woods. On the whole, CCC enrollees were no such men. Some had never even been in a woodlot. In fact, about the only thing that qualified CCC boys for any type of work at all was their need for employment. As a result, Forest Service leaders were asked to "understand their humanitarian role in restoring among the enrollees self-confidence and faith in the future through worthwhile work."[29]

The Forest Service regularly sent inspectors to the camps. It was the job of the inspectors to make sure that camp offices were well organized and that administrators were keeping daily diaries of work activities and accomplishments. Inspectors kept an eye on how camp members got along with army staff. They also noted the general condition of the camp and the organization of its crews. They watched tool supplies, evaluated the condition of vehicles and fire equipment, monitored the health of the men, and made sure the educational program was properly carried out. An inspection report of one CCC camp, Camp Sawyer in the Chequamegon National Forest near Winter, Wisconsin, indicates that 210 men were stationed in camp, that they averaged twenty-nine work details for the previous week, and that 80 percent of the enrollees in the camp worked on forestry projects during the week of inspection.[30]

Local Challenges

Unemployed men living near CCC camps asked the Forest Service to explain why they (the local men) could not be hired to do the kind of work that newly minted CCC boys were not exactly overqualified to perform. The question not only had merit for its thoughtfulness but also put Forest Service officials and CCC workers in an awkward spot, so an appropriate accommodation was made. Accordingly, "Not wanting to create a situation where newly hired city men would march past the homes of unemployed local men to go to work for the CCC, they [the CCC] decided to employ local men at each camp in supervisory capacities wherever practicable."[31] In many instances, local experienced men, or LEM, worked at a CCC camp during the day and returned to their homes at night.

First Two Years

From March 1933 to April 1, 1935, the CCC employed more than a million men. About 940,000 were regular recruits. Others were veterans, and 32,000 were Native Americans. Additionally, LEM such as carpenters, stonemasons, and electricians, along with professional people such as unemployed teachers, foresters, and soil conservation specialists, found work at CCC camps across the country.

The communities near CCC camps benefited economically from the presence of new faces with money in their pockets and a need for supplies. Fechner wrote in a status report to President Roosevelt that "due to the size of the Emergency Conservation Work program and its varied needs, literally thousands of firms have participated in the business created by this undertaking. Nearly all types of materials or supplies which go to make up modern, everyday American Life have been required . . . during the program of Emergency Conservation Work."[32] Any outfit selling food, textiles and clothing, lumber and construction materials, leather goods (especially shoes), and a number of other commodities benefited financially with the CCC around. So too was the CCC a boon for the transportation industry.[33]

FURTHER LEGISLATION

The CCC was originally funded to last two years. It soon became apparent, however, that because the program was so popular with the public and politicians alike, the CCC would require more money to stay in operation beyond 1935. To keep the CCC and other federal relief programs like it going, Congress passed the Emergency Relief Appropriation Act in April 1935, funding the CCC an additional two years through March 31, 1937. With financial security came expansion. By June 30, the CCC had grown to include six hundred thousand enrollees working in 2,916 camps. Furthermore, by 1936 the CCC had become more inclusive, as the age range for admission went from eighteen to twenty-five years old to seventeen to twenty-eight years old. More men and more camps also meant more military men. By the end of 1935, nearly six thousand reserve officers plus another seventy warrant officers found themselves in the CCC.[34]

The 1937 legislation increased the potential term of employment for CCC recruits. Initially, the amount of time a recruit could stay in camp was limited to six months. That changed six months after the creation of the CCC when Roosevelt authorized reenrollment. From that point forward, under the language of the 1937 legislation, aggregate service in the CCC could not, with the exception of exempted personnel, total more than two years.[35]

1937 CCC LEGISLATION

As the years passed and the Depression continued, more legislative action was taken to keep the CCC afloat. Every time Congress acted to prolong the existence of the CCC, changes came to the program. Public Law No. 163, passed by Congress in 1937, extended the life of the CCC.

An Act to establish a Civilian Conservation Corps and for other purposes:

Be it enacted by the Senate and the House of Representatives of the United States of America in Congress assembled, That there is hereby established the Civilian Conservation Corps, hereinafter called the Corps, for the purpose of providing employment, as well as vocational training, for youthful citizens of the United States who are unemployed and in need of employment, and to a limited extent as hereinafter set out, for war veterans and Indians, through the performance of useful public work in connection with the conservation and development of the natural resources of the United States, its territories, and insular possessions. . . . That the provisions of this Act shall continue for the period of three years after July 1, 1937, and no longer.[36]

The Act also included the following provisions:

- At least ten hours a week of general and vocational education should be provided enrollees.

- The salary for the national director of the CCC shall be set at $10,000 a year.

The passage of Public Law No. 163 also brought with it an important name change. Where the CCC had up to this time been officially referred to as the Emergency Conservation Work program, the Civilian Conservation Corps now became the organization's official name. And with a new name came more funding, as Congress authorized another three years' worth of appropriations to keep young Americans at work on the land.

- A cap of three hundred thousand is to be placed on the number of CCC enrollees at any one time, of which no more than thirty thousand can be war veterans.

- Enrollees, with the exception of war veterans, must be unmarried male citizens of the United States between seventeen and twenty-eight years old.

- Enrollments shall be for a period of not less than six months, and reenrollments, with the exception of one mess steward, three cooks, and one leader in each company to not exceed a total term of two years.

- Enrollees may receive a leave of absence to attend an educational institution.

- Compensation will be $30.00 per month. Assistant leaders may receive up to $36.00 per month. Enrollees designated as leaders may receive up to $45.00 per month.

- In addition to monthly compensation, enrollees will be entitled to housing, food, clothing, medical care, and transportation.[37]

Leaders and assistant leaders were designated by the Department of Labor. Many were chosen because they had prior experience in forestry work. Others could work their way into leadership roles such as night watchman, blacksmith helper, carpenter helper, or mess steward. These positions also came with a rating of leader or assistant leader.[38]

ADMINISTRATIVE ORGANIZATION

In 1933, Camp McCoy, located between Sparta and Tomah, was designated as the quartermaster supply base of the CCC in Wisconsin. Quartermaster supply bases provided the uniforms and equipment needed by the CCC to do their work. A year later, Camp McCoy became

TYPICAL DAILY MENU FOR A CCC CAMP

Enrollees in the CCC ate well and ate often. This menu includes the kinds of fare that most camps served.

Breakfast

1-½ boxes of apples

175 individually packaged breakfast food

Wheat cakes with pork sausage (thirty-seven pounds of pork)

One-gallon of syrup

Three pounds of jelly

175 doughnuts or cookies

Five pounds of butter

Six pounds of coffee

175 one-half pints of milk

Dinner

One dozen bunches of green onions

Fifty pounds of roast beef

the headquarters for the Fourteenth CCC Forestry District, and three new buildings and additional warehouse space were added to the camp. The following year, a reorganization took place in which the tenth, twelfth, thirteenth, and fourteenth districts were consolidated into the new Sparta CCC District. The CCC district headquarters at Camp McCoy was then moved to Sparta in the fall of 1935 when it was determined that the facilities at Camp McCoy were inadequate to meet ever-increasing storage demands.

The new facilities in Sparta, however, especially the warehouse space, soon became insufficient as well. The CCC was expanding its ranks

Five no. 10 cans of creamed peas

One dozen bunches of radishes

Four bunches of celery

Fifteen pounds of bread

Five pounds of butter

Three pounds of jam

Six pounds of coffee

Supper

Fifteen gallons of tomato noodle soup with crackers

Thirty pounds of meat loaf

Thirty pounds of fried potatoes

Fifteen pounds of buttered carrots

Fifteen pounds of cabbage salad

Pie or cake

Six pounds of coffee.[39]

quickly, and the amount of supplies needed to maintain its operations in Wisconsin grew proportionally. Instead of building another structure, the government leased storage space from the American Suppliers Company in Sparta.

Every day, administrators and workers at the Sparta CCC Center woke up to find waiting for them the enormous logistical challenge of feeding, clothing, and supplying twenty thousand men in ninety active CCC camps across central and northern Wisconsin. Of the more than two hundred men who worked at the headquarters in Sparta, many were responsible for handling tons of supplies designated for shipment to various CCC camps. Commodities were always coming and going through headquarters, as "the four railroad tracks were loaded to capacity with both empty and full freight cars, as high as 14 cars were handled every day."[40] District staff had a difficult job, made all the more so by being constantly reminded to keep costs down. The task of doing so also fell on the army officer who supervised the mess operation in each CCC camp. This person ordered the various foodstuffs and supervised their preparation, all with a watchful eye on expenditures. In 1933, it cost about thirty-three cents a day to feed a CCC enrollee. As the Depression worsened and the price of food went up, the price soared to forty-six cents a day in 1936.[41] Those relatively small numbers look much larger

THE FOREMAN'S JOB

The title of foreman was given to technical agency supervisory personnel attached to a CCC camp. Different from a foreman working in industry, the duties of a CCC foreman were much broader. As explained in the *CCC Foremanship* handbook, the CCC foreman "must train enrollees not only for production on the job but also for their own general development. Most enrollees have done little manual labor, are not familiar with tools and do not know how to work. Many have had little formal education, and have had poor home training."[43]

The duties of the CCC foreman included the following:

Orientation: Helping new CCC recruits adjust to the routine and atmosphere of the camp.

Supervision: Making sure the job to be done was done properly, safely, and efficiently.

Training: Training enrollees to work efficiently and safely. In addition, the training included leadership development, helping enrollees understand the basic principles of conservation, and providing each enrollee with at least one skill that may appeal to a future employer.

Administration: Planning and organizing the work to be done and ensuring that the necessary materials and equipment were available

when measured against the huge quantities of food CCC enrollees consumed. In June 1937 alone, CCC camps in the Sparta district went through "approximately 88,000 pounds of fresh beef, 8,800 pounds of fresh bread, 100,000 pints of fresh milk, 175,000 pounds of potatoes, and 18,000 pounds of butter."[42]

After the headquarters transfer from Camp McCoy to Sparta, Camp McCoy remained in operation as a conditioning camp. The camp also went through a period of expansion, benefiting from the Works Progress Administration program. Another of FDR's many New Deal initiatives,

for the prescribed work. When other supervisory staff was absent, the foreman should be prepared to take charge of the camp.

Safety Training: A safety training meeting was required twice a month, and the foreman must take an active part in the meetings and set a good example on the importance of safety in all aspects of the camp.

Conservation: The CCC foreman must personally believe in the value of conservation, have a basic knowledge of conservation, know what it is and how it is accomplished, and be willing to share his knowledge and beliefs with CCC enrollees.

Relation with the Public: The CCC foreman should understand well the organization and operation of the program and be willing to readily share this information with the public. He should be ready to explain the nature of the work the enrollees are doing; that they are receiving job training while doing the work and are learning the value of work, self-reliance, and personal care; and are being given the opportunity to participate in general educational offerings. To assure the respect of the public, "all those in supervisory positions must conduct themselves carefully, not only in official business but also in their personal affairs. . . . Rowdy, boisterous conduct, intoxication, frequenting of questionable places of entertainment, slovenly appearance, careless dress, laxity in paying bills, and similar immoral and careless habits . . . will reflect on the whole CCC organization."[44]

the WPA (Works Progress Administration; renamed the Works Projects Administration in 1939) built six new buildings at Camp McCoy. By 1938, Camp McCoy had become the largest physical conditioning site for CCC enrollees in the Midwest. In 1939, when the CCC began to cut its numbers, Camp McCoy went through another change when a new discharge and reception center was constructed there to facilitate the "out-processing" of CCC members.[45]

ORGANIZATIONAL CHALLENGES

Holding positions of executive leadership, army men were in command at CCC camps. Officers' Reserve Corps officers kept order in their camps as they would in infantry units on the battlefield. Officers oversaw educational and training programs and made sure that CCC enrollees were properly fed, housed, and cared for medically. Beneath the officers, a second line of authority included civilian representatives from the Department of Agriculture (in forestry and soil conservation camps) or the Department of the Interior (in camps within state or national parks). These men oversaw building construction and execution of camp purposes and goals. The chain of command in a camp with forestry responsibilities, for example, might run from an army officer to a camp superintendent. Beneath them might be three or four construction foremen, then two or three subforemen, some of whom were LEM.

With so many men from different backgrounds working to satisfy agendas that sometimes competed with each other, feathers were bound to be ruffled. Conflicts between colleagues were inevitable. In the CCC camps in Wisconsin's national forests, tensions mounted between the army and the Forest Service. Problems simmered in these camps for several years until 1940, when a meeting was held in Milwaukee at which CCC personnel from the army and the Forest Service were expected to hash out their differences. Sometimes directives sent from the army and the Forest Service—made independently of each other—unwittingly pitted army and Forest Service staff against one another. So too were the army and Forest Service at odds over what educational opportunities should be offered to camp enrollees, as the branches of service were not in agreement about what skills to teach their charges. Nor did it help that the Forest Service periodically sent inspectors to the CCC camps to rate relations with the army and to ascertain the extent to which the army was cooperating with the Forest Service.[46]

Yet in the end it was not leadership at any administrative level that mattered so much. It was the recruits, the millions of enrollees who put their labor into a cause greater than themselves, and in return came away with more than they could have hoped for. These men are the subject of the next chapter.

4

The CCC Recruit

Dressed in a wrinkled World War I uniform, still reeking of mothballs, he was driven to camp in a stake truck and assigned to a . . . bunk in a barracks where home became "a footlocker and two feet of iron pipe for hanging your coveralls." . . . [A] homesick recruit could only groan at the 6 a.m. bugle and join other skinny, pale youngsters in a day of tree planting, road building or firefighting.[1]

Participation in the CCC was considered a privilege. The CCC offered young men without anything or any direction the opportunity to earn a living and maybe learn a trade. So too did it offer relief to countless families. This fact was one that local agencies were asked to keep in mind when selecting recruits. Unattached, homeless, or transient men were not to be selected. While such men may have been deserving of admission, the mission of the CCC went beyond putting young unemployed men to work. The program was designed to help as many people as possible.

Local agencies largely determined who was in and who was out. Alrine Williamson lived with her family on a Dane County farm during the Great Depression. She wanted to enroll her sons in the CCC, but they were turned away. Alrine's granddaughter, Nancy Williamson, recalled a conversation she had with her grandmother in the mid-1970s when Nancy was working on a high school English project. Nancy wrote:

The government told them [the Williamson family] that their farm in Dane County would provide a livelihood for the boys, as well as the rest of the family during those tough times and that the young men were ineligible to participate in that New Deal program. My grandparents were struggling to pay taxes and bills and make ends meet during the Depression, as was every other farmer they knew. . . .

The portion of a CCC worker's income that came home to the parents would've helped ease my grandparents' struggle considerably. The harsh emotions Grandma felt [toward Franklin D. Roosevelt] were intensified when World War II came. The sons that had been excluded from conservation service for their country were quickly required to enter military service without delay, then sent to far-off Italy, North Africa, and the South Pacific.[2]

African Americans in the CCC

CCC recruitment policies prohibited any denial of acceptance based on race. Thus, some of the first CCC camps were integrated with a scattering of young African American men. By 1935, however, a "complete segregation of colored and white enrollees" had taken place.[3]

Of the more than three million young men enrolled in the CCC from 1933 to 1942, about 250,000 were African Americans assigned to nearly 150 all-black CCC companies. Black enrollees did the same work as their white CCC counterparts—they planted trees, fought fires, improved parks, built roads, and much more. In the 1930s, about 10 percent of the US population was African American—and roughly 10 percent of the CCC enrollment was as well. Racism was rampant. In many states, especially in the South, potential black enrollees were passed over in favor of white men. Some of the communities surrounding black CCC camps were hostile to black recruits. Many army officers and Forest Service supervisors harbored racist attitudes toward blacks. And even in all-black camps, young African American men found it difficult or impossible to assume positions of leadership.

Even though the law creating the CCC included language forbidding racial discrimination, program director Robert Fechner maintained that "segregation is not discrimination."[4] In a letter to the president of the National Association for the Advancement of Colored People, written September 21, 1935, Fechner justified his position by claiming that:

> the law enacted by Congress setting up the Emergency Conservation Work specifically indicated that there should be no discrimination because of color. I have faithfully endeavored to obey the spirit and the letter of the law. . . . While segregation has been the general policy, it has not been inflexible, and we have a number of companies containing a small number of Negro enrollees. I am satisfied that the Negro enrollees themselves prefer to be in companies composed exclusively of their own race. . . . This segregation is not discrimination and cannot be so construed. The Negro companies are assigned to the same types of work, have identical equipment, are served the same food, and have the same quarters as white enrollees.[5]

Camps continued to be segregated by race until the CCC was disbanded in 1942.

NATIVE AMERICANS IN THE CCC

In 1933, enlistment coverage in the CCC was expanded to include Native Americans. Eventually, some eighty thousand Native Americans were paid to help improve conditions on their reservations. Native Americans in the CCC, who were enrolled in the CCC-ID, or the Civilian Conservation Corps-Indian Division, mainly worked on reservations building roads, improving water resources, and controlling erosion. Native Americans, like LEM, were allowed to return home in the evening instead of living in a camp. Tribal councils worked with CCC administrators to identify and implement Native American CCC work projects. In addition, the work had an important quality of Indian self-determination, as an editorial in the CCC-ID's newsletter, *Indians at Work*, included these words: "No previous undertaking in Indian Service has so largely been the Indians' own under-taking, as the emergency conservation work."[6]

Clothing Allowance

The army provided clothing for CCC enrollees. Much of it was surplus left-over from World War I. Recruits were given clothing for work and for dress. Typically, each man received two dress summer uniforms and two dress winter uniforms. Dress uniforms worn in winter were spruce green. Those worn in summer were khaki. Stripes on the uniforms depicted leadership positions—two stripes: assistant leader; three stripes: leader. Recruits were also given a poncho for rainy weather, one black tie, two work uniforms, one pair of work shoes and one pair of dress shoes, two bath towels, a shaving kit with toothbrush, two pairs of socks, two pairs of underwear, and two olive drab handkerchiefs.[7]

In northern regions, cold-weather clothing was handed out. Long underwear, an overcoat, overshoes, mittens, a winter hat and in some instances heavy boots, windbreakers, and even snowshoes were available for men working where the snow was deep.[8]

The CCC Handbook

The CCC national office provided each CCC enrollee with an official hand-book. Enrollees could open their handbooks and find information on the following topics, listed by chapter title:

- What's It All About (purposes of the program)

- How It All Began (history of the legislation)

- How It Operates (who is in charge and what are their responsibilities)

- Mother Nature (why conservation of nature resources is important)

- Pick and Shovel (forty hours of work per week)

- Pay Day Every Month ($30.00 per month, $25.00 goes home)

- It's Not All Work (many recreational opportunities)

- Life and Limb (safety measures are important)

- To Your Health (a doctor in every camp)

- Learning to Earn (many educational opportunities)

- Toeing the Line (discipline is important)

- Going to Town (with permission, visits away from camp possible)

- Religious Activities (church services available)

- Manners-Courtesy (learn to say "yes, sir")

- The Camp Community (connecting to the nearby communities, maintaining the local camp)

- Getting Along (the need to share and care)

- Tell It to Your Folks (write letters home)

When a recruit had a question about anything related to what he should be doing in camp, how he should be doing it, and what were the consequences of failing to do it, he turned to the CCC handbook for answers. For instance, if an enrollee tired of the work and considered leaving camp, he would learn on page 27 that there were consequences for desertion. Alternatively, if a CCC man wanted a "second hitch" in the CCC, he turned to page 51, where he read: "To be eligible for re-enrollment, a junior must be physically fit, must be within the . . . age limit, must not have served more than 18 months . . . must be unmarried, and his performance of work satisfactory to both the company commander and the project Superintendent."[9]

HAPPY DAYS

For CCC boys living in tents far from the closest town and farther still from home, reading was more than a pastime. It was how they stayed in touch with the world beyond the marginal limits of their camp. News was essential. Shortly after the CCC was established, a national camp newspaper was launched on May 20, 1933. The semi-official newspaper was called *Happy Days*. Published in Washington, DC, the paper went out to CCC camps across the country. Ray Hoyt was the managing editor and Theodore Arter Jr. the business manager. Arter had served in World War I on the staff of the army newspaper *Stars and Stripes*, so he had a good feel for the kind of writing that young men away from home and congregated in groups would find of interest. Indeed, its first issue proclaimed that *Happy Days* had no particular policy except that of "being of good cheer and giving you the dope."[10] *Happy Days* included national news and news from CCC camps around the United States.

Happy Days invited material from its CCC readers. Newspaper staff emphasized that the paper belonged to CCC enrollees, and they were welcome to contribute to it. The paper solicited, for example, selections of poetry to print in the section "Brother Can You Spare a Rhyme" (a riff on the phrase oft-heard during the Depression, "Brother can you spare a dime?"). One of the more interesting published poems was titled (after the Twenty-Third Psalm) "The 221st Company Psalm." From a camp in New Jersey, a CCC member waxed:

Roosevelt's my Shepard, I shall not want;
He maketh me to lie down on straw mattresses;
He leadeth me inside a mess hall;
He restoreth to me a job.[11]

Local Camp Newspapers

Happy Days encouraged its readership to replicate its model in their camps. *Happy Days* staff tried to provide a blueprint both in the quality and tone of its writing that others could readily follow. As a result, local camp newspapers flourished. From 1933 to 1942, more than five thousand local camp newspapers were printed across the range of the CCC.[12]

To find out about daily CCC camp activities, the camp newspaper was the place to look. Written and edited by the CCC boys themselves (some of whom were given an introduction to journalism by an educational advisor), the camp newspaper, usually published once a month, contained articles by the staff—the camp doctor, for example—as well as stories, poetry, and essays written by members of the CCC.

Many Wisconsin CCC camps had local newspapers. Here is an excerpt from the first issue of the *Nu-Wud-Nus: Edited on the banks of the Little Ole Wisconse*, the camp newspaper for CCC Camp New Wood. It is dated December 6, 1934. Camp New Wood, manned by Company 2616, opened near Merrill on September 6, 1934. It closed in 1935.[13]

Nu-Wud-Nus Makes Debut

Camp New Wood, Company 2616 of the 12th District, with this issue makes its first bow in CCC journalistic circles. The paper is published once a month and is mimeographed at the Merrill High School. Each subsequent issue, it is hoped, will show marked improvement.

As *Nu-Wud-Nus* is the Camp paper, every enrollee is duly appointed a reporter. No newspaper is a success without news from and about everybody. *Nu-Wud-Nus* will not be an exception. The old gag about no news being good news is all wet in press circles. There must be news, and the men of this company must ferret it out and give this paper that news. Cooperation is an essential in community news projects. Just one item of news from every man in this company would make *Nu-Wud-Nus* the largest paper in the district.[14]

Local camp newspapers like *Nu-Wud-Nus* printed everything from local gossip to serious articles to various kinds of jokes. This example comes from a local paper out of Camp Connors Lake in Phillips, Wisconsin:

Windy Pete

One morning when I lived in Alaska, the thermometer registered 90 below. I was heating water. I got it too hot and took it outside to cool. While I stood there the water froze so fast that the ice was still warm when I brought it inside.[15]

Sometimes serious concerns, such as those around safety, were expressed humorously in camp newspapers. Here is an example from the *Dugout*, the paper produced by Company 2625 of Camp Hales Corners:

They missed the turn
The car was wizzin'
The fault was her'n
The funeral—his'n.[16]

Local papers were organized by topic in much the same way as they are today. A reader can get a good feel for this by looking through old issues of the *Camp Irving Weekly*, the local paper produced by enrollees in CCC Company 658 stationed at Camp Irving in Black River Falls. The *Camp Irving Weekly* had an active readership and reporting staff, as the paper was published weekly—different from most local CCC papers that were monthly publications. The six-page publication included the following departments:

Editorial: Interesting happenings from around the camp. A story ran about the camp's truckdrivers traveling to Sparta for a one-day safety school. The writer concluded with, "So it can be seen that a worthwhile day was had by all; (not forgetting the oyster stew)."

Biographical Sketches: Background information about enrollees. One two-page article began: "The writing of this biography will undoubtedly be my farewell address as well, as there is no doubt that the victim of this article will make every attempt to annihilate me in the very near future after the publication of this little bit of truth. But nevertheless, here goes."

Sports: The November 6, 1936, issue includes a detailed plan for an upcoming camp football tournament. It reads, "Each barrack will have two teams, one from each end of the barrack. . . . The game will be run with a six man team and frequent substitutions will be permitted."

Soil Conservation: As Camp Irving was a soil conservation camp, a page was devoted to work in this area, including an essay written by the paper's editor about the dangers of wind erosion: "In the spring of 1935 . . . millions of tons of soil were lifted from the great wheat fields of the West and distributed over many states. Some of this soil was carried thousands of miles."

All in Fun: Some attempts at humor.[17]

CLIPS FROM THE *KICKAPOOJIAN*

The Camp Gays Mills newspaper, the *Kickapoojian*, ran creative and ironic contributions from its writers. Some of the better examples are listed here.

S is for the stew they always feed us
H is for the home we seldom see
O is for the onions and our taste buds
V is for the coming victory
E is for the end of our enlistment
L is for the last you'll see of me
Put them all together and they spell s-h-o-v-e-l, the symbol
   of the CCC.

Our Alma Mater
Oh, the coffee that they serve you they say is mighty fine
It heals cuts and bruises and tastes like iodine
I don't want no more of the CCC, gee I wanna go home
The biscuits in the mess hall are said to taste divine
But one rolled off the table and killed a pal of mine
I don't want no more of the CCC, gee I wanna go home
The wages that they pay you can buy you paradise
They last for just one roll of a barrack's game of dice
I don't want no more of the CCC, gee I wanna go home
The room and board are furnished along with army clothes
And when I get back home I will have no more such woes
Oh, I don't want no more of the CCC, gee I wanna go home.[18]

The *Rusketeer* was the camp newspaper for Camp Rusk in Glen Flora. These are excerpts from the paper's first edition, published September 1935:

Camp Improvements

Through the combined efforts of the officers and enrollees, Camp Rusk is gradually being transformed from the most dilapidated camp in the district to one that will in a short time become beautiful and comfortable.

The camp carpenters quickly installed a large ice-box in the kitchen, which adequately keeps the perishable food in good condition. Shortly after the refrigeration projects, an efficient and modern grease trap was built. At the same time the entire drainage system was improved. Plans were drawn to improve the general appearance of the camp, so instead of being an eyesore it would be a sight for sore eyes. A four-foot terrace will be built along each building. Graveled paths and cross paths will lead into Main Street. Neat strips of sod outlining the paths will lend an air of quiet beauty and cleanliness.

Much has been accomplished, but much more needs to be accomplished. The rookies proved a great asset and their coming on January 30 spurred the necessary work. When the improvements are completed, Camp Rusk can hold up its head among other camps.

Camp Projects

The projects that are lined up for the future will offer enough work for the one-hundred and ninety odd boys this winter and coming spring. The building of the new road to camp is one of the many projects that is being worked on now. The lake and stream improvement project under the direction of Mr. Moreau is another project in effect. The road will be completed in a short while if dry weather prevails, but so far rain has hindered the building of the road considerably. With two tractors and a double shift the camp has made considerable time even against the element menace.

The forestry might in the near future start brushing out a game refuge somewhere in the vicinity. This will be a very interesting job for any fellow who has been in the city all his life. The lake and stream crew has been doing a lot of work around Ingram, but when the weather gets a little colder, the crew will be shifted to another project. Roadside cleanup, telephone line work, and cutting cedar poles will be the other winter jobs.[19]

It is worth noting that the costs of producing the *Rusketeer* were covered by local businesses. CCC enrollees were potential customers of the places that supported the paper. Graves Grocery, Rusk County Hardware, Pioneer National Bank, Ladysmith Bakery, Unique Theater, Wherbatt Shoe Shop, Ladysmith Pharmacy, Ladysmith Milk Producers Cooperative Association, and the *Ladysmith News* all chipped in to make the *Rusketeer* possible.

In many cases, the camp newspapers were as much an achievement as any of the conservation projects completed by the CCC. Alfred Emile Cornebise sums up local CCC camp newspaper activity this way: "Though the papers varied widely in quality, given the limitations of the mimeographed form, many functioned at an impressively high level and were characterized by vivacity, style, originality, and imagination, and many excellent editors and writers emerged."[20]

Getting to Camp

On the Way to Camp Rusk, Glen Flora

The trip to a CCC camp was a long one for many recruits. This CCC camp news article from the *Rusketeer* gives a good description of what it was like for an enrollee to reach his final destination. In capturing his journey from Milwaukee to Ladysmith, the author writes:

Many impatient young men hurried and scurried here and there to arrive at the Milwaukee Depot at 6:00 p.m. . . . There they waited until 7:30 before the train pulled out. Leaving the depot, we traveled through the main part of Milwaukee until we arrived at the outskirts of the town. From there on we saw nothing but grass and farms. We also passed through many small junctions and factory cities such as Oshkosh and Stevens Point.

We arrived about 4:30 a.m. in Ladysmith, all stiff and sore from the uncomfortable ride. Most of the fellows left the train to look over the town or to go to a restaurant, being hungry from the long ride. We left Ladysmith in route to Glen Flora, where the trucks awaited to take us to camp.[21]

On the Way to Camp Sailor Lake, Fifield

Lawrence Kant recalled his trip to and his first days at Camp Sailor Lake located near Fifield, Wisconsin, in much the same way that young men like him from across the country chronicled their own voyages in camp newspapers and letters home to family. Kant writes:

As our train pulled into Fifield, someone shouted, "Sailor Lake." Well not quite. Army trucks were standing by for the 11 mile ride to the projected camp. It didn't take long before a familiar voice cried out loud and clear: "Sailor Lake." Sure enough; there it was, situated on a low swampy mud plat; a dismal picture, indeed.

Sailor Lake is located roughly 75 miles south of Ashland . . . [and] is part of the Nicolet National Park, known as the lower Flambeau district, which is composed of 38,000 acres.

Fifield is located at the junction of Highways 13 and 70. Loss of the lumber industry had reduced its population to a village status, and most of the boys did their shopping in nearby Phillips or Park Falls, having populations of several thousand.

Our first day in camp was a nightmare. After a light lunch (the mess tent stood in the mud), came the familiar lecture on our projected contribution toward the development of a national forestry program to enhance our environment.

Then we were assigned to tents: 8 men, 8 cots, and a stove. The cots rested on boards, but the mud in the tent was ankle deep. Most of us were dead tired and thus decided to get a bit of shuteye. We unlaced our shoes (the leather is reversed on these army shoes, with the smooth side inside and the rough side on the outside; the leather absorbed water like a soft sponge). We removed our feet from the shoes in the mud and slipped under the blankets, clothes and all.

The following day several men dug a 12 foot well for drinking water. The well water was poured into a canvas bag, which had a spigot on the bottom. The canvas bag hung between two trees.

The third day the men were split up. Two-thirds went with the forestry department and were assigned to brush cleaning detail, to pave the way for the fall, tree planting season. The men left with the Army department in charge and began leveling off the ground around the camp and filling in the low spots, of which there were many.[22]

GREETINGS FROM PRESIDENT ROOSEVELT

Franklin Delano Roosevelt was president during the entire operational lifespan of the CCC. There is no man with whom the CCC is more closely associated, as it was FDR who brought it swiftly into being and oversaw its successes. He took his role as the de facto leader of the CCC very seriously. FDR wrote to new CCC recruits:

> I welcome the opportunity to extend a greeting to the men who constitute the Civilian Conservation Corps. It is my belief that what is being accomplished will conserve our national resources, create future national wealth and prove of moral and spiritual value, not only to those of you who are taking part, but to the rest of the country as well. . . .
>
> I want to congratulate you on the opportunity you have, and to extend to you my appreciation for the hearty cooperation you have given the movement, so vital a step in the nation's fight against depression, and to wish you a pleasant, wholesome and constructive stay in the CCC.[23]

MEMORIES OF CCC RECRUITS

Just as the land still remembers what the CCC did to save it during the darkest days of the Depression, so does the memory of the CCC live on in the minds of those who are descended from its recruits. In the following passages, family members of those who served in the CCC offer their own memories and recollections of what the CCC meant to those who worked the land under its guidance.

William and August Bongers
Eleanore Schuetz remembered her two uncles, William (Bill) and August (Gus) Bongers, who both served in the CCC camp near Tomahawk. Eleanore wrote:

> My grandmother (a German immigrant in 1896) became a widow at age 32, in 1923. Her husband was killed dynamiting stumps to clear more of their farm land and she was left with four children, ages 13, 12, 10 and 4. She did whatever she could to keep her family fed and to keep the land. As the children grew, they all pitched in to help pay the bills.
>
> Both of my uncles became young men during the Depression and they both joined the CCC. They were both at Camp Tomahawk CCC Company 1608 (S-84). Uncle Bill, the older of the two brothers, did not like the regimented military style of the camp, but he was happy to have work and to be able to send money home to his family. He talked about playing ball in his free time, going to dances and movies. He also talked about planting trees in the New Wood area [now the New Wood Wildlife Area]. He didn't much care for the tree planting. I believe he was in on some of the firefighting activities also. He must have taken some classes offered through the CCC as he became a very proficient mechanic and carpenter.
>
> Uncle Gus had attended Tomahawk High School and graduated in about 1936, and joined the CCC about 1937. He enjoyed the military lifestyle and eventually went into the army and later was a very active National Guardsmen. During the War he was in a tank unit and awarded the Purple Heart for action in Italy.
>
> Uncle Bill was reluctant to talk about his memories of any of his early childhood or the difficult Depression days. He rode the rails and traveled all over trying to find jobs: on threshing crews, apple harvest

in Washington state, work on the world's fair in California, work on the Hoover Dam and in the CCC camp.[24]

Camp Tomahawk was located on the corner of McCord Road and Highway 8, west of Tomahawk. It was established in November 1933 and closed in November 1941. During the summer of 1934, a carpentry and building course was conducted at the camp. A log headquarters building for the Forestry Service resulted from the course. Other activities conducted at the camp included lake surveys, construction of fire lookout towers, fighting forest fires, constructing truck trails and fire breaks, and working on the elimination of gooseberry shrubs in order to prevent the spread of white pine blister rust. Today the once vibrant CCC camp is a grove of trees.[25]

Deforest Waid

Paul Waid recalled some of the experiences his father, Deforest Waid, had as a CCC recruit stationed at Camp New Wood:

Deforest Waid served in the CCC at Camp New Wood near Merrill. COURTESY OF PAUL WAID

> My dad came from a very poor family in the Pine River area of Waushara County. He had to leave home at age 14 and for a time worked on area farms. I'm not sure of the exact year he went into the CCC. His job there was driving a truck and planting trees. Very few boys knew how to drive then, so he got the job.
>
> When he was discharged from the CCC, he only had the clothes on his back. He was hitchhiking home when a farmer picked him up. The farmer asked him where he was headed and my dad said, Pine River. The farmer asked if he needed work. My dad said he did and the farmer hired him.
>
> He worked for the farmer for some time, and fell in love with the farmer's daughter, Lola Stevenson. When World War II came along, he married her. They honeymooned in Massachusetts for a month

and then my dad was shipped to North Africa, then to Italy and on to France. My dad and his new bride (my mother) didn't see each other for three years.

My dad recalled how hard they all worked while in the CCC, but he also said he was glad to have a job. All the CCC boys got along pretty good, because they were all in the same boat, with no job before the CCC. Thanks to his job driving trucks in the CCC, this became his job in the army.[26]

Howard James Hunn

Jeanne Evert has these memories of her father's experience with the CCC. About Howard James Hunn, Evert writes:

My father, Howard James Hunn, worked with the CCC for eight years after graduating from the University of Illinois with a B.S. degree in Landscape Architecture. His schooling included several years at the University of Wisconsin–Madison after completing high school at the Milwaukee School of Agriculture.

Howard James Hunn, a landscape architect, served in the CCC and designed several CCC camps across the country, including Camp Rib Mountain near Wausau.
COURTESY OF JEANNE EVERT

The CCC sites where he worked included Honey Creek Parkway in Milwaukee, sites in Madison, Rib Mountain Park near Wausau, as well as in Creston, Louisiana. Many areas at these sites were designed by Howard and then built by CCC boys.

For a time, Howard was the Superintendent at the Rib Mountain site.[27]

Anthony J. Caffrey

Gerald Brock recalled a story his uncle, his mother's brother, Anthony J. Caffrey, shared about Caffrey's CCC experiences. Caffrey was in his twenties in the 1930s. As a child, Caffrey suffered from tuberculosis, and staff at the sanitarium thought working at a CCC camp in the north might be good for his health. He was assigned to a CCC camp near Rhinelander. At the time of this incident, Caffrey had some supervisory responsibilities:

> One night the men got into some canned heat, which was basically wax with alcohol. The men were getting drunk by chewing the wax. Two of them got into a knife fight and my uncle had to run out there and break it up in the woods in the middle of the night under the bright moon. He says he was frightened, but he stopped the fight. He was a tough guy.[28]

5

The Spoolman Journals

J. (John) Allen Spoolman was born December 23, 1913. As a child, he and his family lived in Birnamwood, Wisconsin, before moving to Ashland when he was ten or eleven. Spoolman graduated from high school in Ashland in 1931 and was enrolled for a brief time at Northland College in Ashland before working for the CCC during the years 1934 and 1935. Spoolman was an amateur artist and aspired to become a writer. He kept a detailed diary of his time working as a CCC enrollee at Camp Pigeon Lake, not far from Drummond, Wisconsin, and about thirty-five miles from Ashland. The following are excerpts from Spoolman's writings, which give us a rare inside look at the day-to-day activity of a CCC enrollee.

Tuesday, November 13, 1934, 10:00 p.m.
Had the job I like today. Shwagur sent me about a mile back to burn two piles of stumps and logs that hadn't burned. So I spent the day alone.

Wednesday, November 14, 9:00 p.m.
Well, I hit a good job yesterday and today. Probably hold through tomorrow and maybe longer. I cleaned up those two bad piles [of brush and logs] slick as a whistle, too. Instead of burning them, instead I dragged the logs back and hid them in the brush. More economical, efficient and less energy on the long run.

Wind howling and ice on the lake. Winter coming on for sure.

I'm just a number now—CCC-107992.

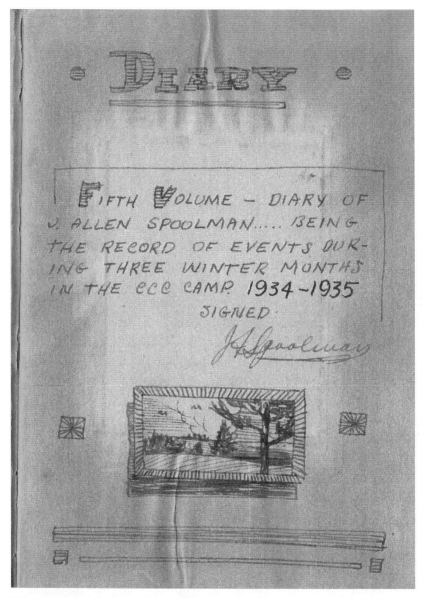

The cover of one of J. Allen Spoolman's CCC journals. COURTESY OF SCOTT SPOOLMAN

Tues. Nov. 13. 10:00 P.M.

Almost time for the
lights to go. Was over at
the Cantine helping Red
harmonize with the guitar
Had the job I like to-
day. Shwaiger sent me
about a mile back to
burn two piles of stumps
and logs that hadn't
burned. So I spent the
day alone. The time sure
travelled fast - too fast,
as I missed the truck
tonight and came in
with Pollack's crew.
Painted up Ben-
edict's trunk for num-
ber one, and have three
or four lined up. It
looks like I'll be able
to square up a few

A journal entry from November 13. COURTESY OF SCOTT SPOOLMAN

Wednesday, December 5, 9:15 p.m.
Wading around in two feet of snow and it's plenty cold, too. Winter's here for sure. It seemed to come quick this year. Had good weather up until the last of November.

Thursday, December 6, 9:00 p.m.
Temperature down to sub-zero this morning—12 below. I took a little walk back in the woods this afternoon and it was like a fairyland.

Thirty men are being transferred Saturday to three other camps. Then, with 53 leaving at the end of the month it will look like a new camp.

Monday, December 10, 9:00 p.m.
Started on the camp road today, finishing what O'Bomdovitch and Acey started a couple of months ago. We'll be through with that though this week; I wonder what job we'll get next.

Monday, December 17, 9:25 p.m.
We have inherited a radio. Belongs to someone across the aisle. It's good to hear music in the shack instead of swearing and yelling.

Douglas failed to show up last night and hasn't shown up yet. Looks like curtains for him. Second offense.

Tuesday, December 18, 9:30 p.m.
Fine snow fell nearly all day, but not heavy enough to stay in from work. We took the final exam in First Aid tonight. I'll get my certificate. Might come in handy.

Few more days before Christmas leave.

Sunday, December 23, 9:30 p.m.
Well, today I turned twenty-one. Just what it means I'm not sure. Time will tell. It's another milestone anyhow.

Sunday, December 30, 9:30 p.m.
Another idle day in camp. By borrowing a dime from Ole . . . I was able to take in the show in the mess hall. Best acting and all round show I've seen for a long time. "Man's Castle" name of it. Spencer Tracy taking the tough role and adopting a homeless girl.

Monday, January 7, 1935, 9:15 p.m.
I'm running a compass line for a timber survey, which isn't so much fun without snowshoes in three feet of snow. Green asked for high school graduates for the job, and Walt and I were the only ones on the crew who could brag about that so we got the job. If I can learn how to use the compass, I may be set with a job that might bring advancement.

Tuesday, January 8, 9:15 p.m.
Boy, this new job is something, wallowing through three feet of snow with a crust just strong enough to make you think it will hold, but then down to your hips. That's torture, but it's worth it if I'll get a chance for the job during the summer. Kurt's been added to the survey crew. I hit the section marker corner pretty close this morning, which was amazing considering the haywire compass outfit I had.

Wednesday, January 9, 9:00 p.m.
We walked three-quarters of a mile after leaving the truck, hoofed up two miles, and hit the brush after ten. But in spite of that and the rotten weather—just plain miserable, as big Ed put it, we made over fifty two-chains [a chain is 66 feet long] by noon coming out on Lake Owen. From there we chained off to the opposite shore, cut back across, over one end of an island and landed up in a little bayou where we built our fire under some balsam to toast our sandwiches.

After a wet dinner, we chained back to the track, finishing the section [640 acres]. The snow alternated with sleet and rain, making just about everything from cap to feet, wet.

Friday, January 11, 10:30 p.m.
We had the real job today. We laid out 60 chains all day and all I had to do was call the chains and furnish pickets. Kurt breaks trail. Dene runs compass and chain, while my official capacity is "rear chain man." I holler "stick." Dene hollers "stuck." I holler "four chain." Dene answers "six chain." I pick up my cruiser's ax, mosey along, spot a likely tree for a picket, hack it down, trim it up, and stand around waiting for Dene to drag out the length of the chain, then the same thing over except the advance of numbers by two.

Friday, January 18, 10:20 p.m.

Slim and I got orders to line another forty this morning, so after dinner we dug us up a couple pair of snowshoes. It makes all the difference in the world on the job. Just like walking along the top of water after wading. It was a treat after wallowing for days through snow as high as our hips. Slim sure looked a sight navigating thru the brush with his six foot-five of up and down.

Tuesday, January 22, 9:00 p.m.

We worked today, but it was plenty cold. Fourteen below this afternoon. Slim and I finished the second forty this morning and started on the third after dinner. It looks like an all winter job as Fred let the remark drop that they were going to try to get as many forties done as they could.

Speaking of temperature, it's around twenty below now, so there probably will be no work call tomorrow—unless it moderates before then.

Wednesday, January 23, 9:40 p.m.

We laid around another morning today, making a short day. It was thirty-six below. It's still about twenty below, so we get another half day off tomorrow. As long it's only a half a day at a time, it's okay. A whole day off means work on Saturday morning.

Thursday, January 24, 9:30 p.m.

Another half a day of work. So far the temperature has been just right. Too cold to work in the morning, but not in the afternoon. And as long as a half day is counted as a whole day, we'll still be able to leave on Friday night.

Saturday, January 26, 8:30 p.m.

We were called out on a fire call yesterday morning. The Russ-Owen lumber company roundhouse caught fire around seven o'clock and by the time we got there, shortly before eight, she was flat. There were a couple of trucks and three locomotives destroyed in it.

Thursday, January 31, 9:30 p.m.
Another pay day and another slew of rookies. Ten from Washburn and thirty from Superior.

Slim and I were put on a saw today. Just like on the survey, his "eagle eye" versus the compass in placing trees. If he falls a popple anywhere near a pine, or hangs it up, that's a score for me. And vice versa. Only I can't hope to ever win verbally from him.

Friday, February 1, 10:20 p.m.
There's a long distance between bulling pulp logs and reading a compass. We were doing that for a couple hours this morning. First we opened up a skid trail to the road, then we piled pulp, then after dinner we sawed again.

Monday, February 4, 9:15 p.m.
More warm weather today and a tough day throwing pulp logs around. Slim and I will be two happy lads when we get that old job back again. It wouldn't be anything more than occasional lifting if it weren't for the snow and the warm weather. The two combine nicely to soak the clothes and mittens. It's snowing again now and if it turns colder may change to a blizzard.

Tuesday, February 5, 8:30 p.m.
Another hard day toting pulp around. If a fellow did that very much he'd sure develop a pair of shoulders. Right now mine are as tender as a sun-burned back.

Monday, February 11, 9:30 p.m.
Slim and I were on the saw again today, with a rookie for a swamper. We sure kept him hopping, too.

Friday, February 15, 10:45 p.m.
Slim and I sawed bolts yesterday afternoon and most of today. Our swamper, Ed, seems to want to go into the kitchen since he began bulling pulp. These rookies have a hard time getting into the harness.

A photo of J. Allen Spoolman included with his journal. COURTESY OF SCOTT SPOOLMAN

Monday, February 18, 8:30 p.m.
More tree falling, only must have had an off day today, because everything happened from hanging 'em up, smashing pines, to having one
fall backwards. I put a nice big popple in a "Y" of a nice big birch, then
Slim chopped the nice big birch down and put them both on a nice
little pine. Then he argued the rest of the afternoon that the whole
thing was my fault.

Tuesday, February 19, 8:45 p.m.
There are rumors flying about the camp being split in the spring.
Some say into three parts, others say in half.

Tuesday, February 26, 8:30 p.m.
Something like 30 below zero this morning, but due to a clear sky and
no wind, we worked anyhow. From 45 cuts this morning, we built 107
by 3:45. Swell day to work after the sun got up.

Thursday, March 7, 9:30 p.m.
Peloquinn dropped a hint this morning that I might get the library
[job] after the first of April. May be just another bubble though.

Monday, March 11, 9:00 p.m.
Another change in jobs today. Still Slim and I are together. We got
called off the crew this morning to go on road traverse with Mac. And
is it fun compared with sawing for the terrible Frenchman.

Tuesday, March 12, 9:30 p.m.
Another day on the road traverse. We rode to the other end this
morning and chained back. At noon we linked up to that road I
worked on . . . last fall. . . . There's a half mile left to do tomorrow.
After that I don't know, but I'm hoping.

Monday, March 25, 9:25 p.m.
The place is lit up for a change with street lights, even lights in the
cans [toilets].

Slim and I got our feet plenty wet today on the job. There are some places in the woods that are pretty bare.

Tuesday, March 26, 9:00 p.m.
Another day done and more snow gone. Some thirty are being transferred sometime next week, but that's all anyone knows definitely around here.

Sunday, March 31, 4:00 p.m.
Saturday morning I was on police detail, wandering around spearing cigarette packages, beer bottles, whiskey bottles, snuff boxes, match boxes, reminiscent of summer days at Brinks. Speaking of Brinks [a CCC side camp], I expect to be there again tomorrow. They posted a call for a 25-man side camp Saturday morning so I (and Slim) went and signed up. Foolish? I guess so. Ditching a good job, plus the possibility of getting the library job to go back to the barrens. Won't be there more than a month, I think. We'll either kill rabbits or burn brush.

Monday, April 1, 9:00 p.m. [at the Brinks side camp]
Well, we are back in God's country (God's forgotten country). We packed up this morning and rolled in about noon. The place looks bare without the tents. And it's been brushed over. The old mess hall looks different than what it did last time I saw it. Something nice about eating and sleeping in the same building though. Tomorrow we burn brush.

Wednesday, April 3, 8:30 p.m.
Slim's been feeling rotten today. We've been burning brush about a half hour's ride from camp. I think the smoke and heat is what's been getting Slim.

It's been a cross between spring and winter. Winter at night and spring in the daytime.

Monday, April 29, 9:00 p.m.
No work today because of—snow!

Tuesday, April 30, 9:30 p.m.
Another payday come and gone. Tomorrow, according
to the latest, 50 men move in from Cable. War vets I guess.
It'll be a hell of a mess around here then. Hope we get back
to Drummond pretty soon. The snow is almost gone again.
Last time I hope.

Monday, May 6, 9:15 p.m.
Peloquinn said I was sure of getting the library job after June 30th,
and I found out for the first time that the job carries a $36.00 rating.
Not bad. That sort of changes my outlook. I can even see myself
staying until December now.

Sunday, May 12, 9:30 p.m.
The first detail from Moose River came in tonight, and we'll be
leaving tomorrow or Tuesday.

Tuesday, May 14, 9:00 p.m. [back to Camp Pigeon Lake]
Well, back to the old camp grounds. We pulled in last night after putting in a long day's work in the brush. The boys from Moose
River were putting up tents as we pulled out. I found a hole in [bar-
racks] number 5 and moved in. So Brinks once more recedes in my
memory.

Wednesday, May 15, 10:45 p.m.
I peeled 64 pulp sticks, nine above yesterday.

Friday, May 17, 10:00 p.m.
She was a pretty hot one today. I got a cross between a sunburn and
a tan. I got the booby prize as a pulp peeler. I got 60 today, which was
the low score. Don't know what old Tom'll do about me if I keep that
up. Get rid of me, I hope.

Tuesday, May 21, 6:00 p.m.
Two more days of pulp peeling, after finally hitting the 70
mark today I feel a little more accomplished. Now comes the

mosquitoes. Last night at baseball practice they were thick
enough to make resistance.

Wednesday, May 22, 10:30 p.m.
The crew went sort of berserk today with dippy Tom Tolman
leading the race with 156 sticks. Some record. Even I hauled off
and peeled 90. That blood blister that popped on my second fin-
ger held me down by at least 10. Cooled off a bit, which scared the
mosquitoes out anyhow.

Sunday, May 26, 12:00 p.m.
Well, just a little better than a month and I'll be in the library. A gent's
job with spare time to type, write, read or swim. It'll mean most of
my weekends will have to be spent in camp, but that's for the best
too, because Saturdays and Sundays at home don't see much accomplished. I'll be saving money . . . and getting six bucks more.

Wednesday, May 29, 9:30 p.m.
Morgan and I worked with Thornbury on the camp survey this morning, then about 10:30 when we'd finished, I started on the map down
at the Forestry Headquarters.
    Johnny gave me a haircut tonight, so I feel a little less crummy. I
sure needed it.

Friday, May 31, 8:25 p.m.
I start in the library Monday, so Peloquinn told me.

Friday, May 31, 10:30 p.m.
White collar jobs have been coming my way by pairs lately. I finished
the camp area map . . . today, then checked out of the Forestry in
favor of a "soft job" plus six much needed more dollars. Yup, begins to
look at last as though my days in the field are over.

Saturday, June 1, 9:00 p.m.
First half day in the library. . . . Reading, writing and swimming
are my "pass-times" for the summer. Reading *Up the Years from
Bloomsbury*, George Arliss' autobiography now.

It's good to be boss of a room, have a desk. Only one thing'd make it perfect. Have my bunk in the little cubby corner over there, occupied by Peloquinn now. That would polish it up smoothly.

Tuesday, June 4, 8:00 p.m.
Rainy day with all the crews in camp, which meant a busy day for me.

I've read more on this job than I did in three months before. Probably go through that whole shelf of new books before long.

Tuesday, June 11, 11:00 a.m.
Nothing much new on this job. Just checking books in and out, and playing pool. I'll have to cut down on the pool, especially since I'm starting to dream about it at night.

Friday, June 14, 9:45 p.m.
Well, I spend most of my spare time on the lakeshore now, with my little black friend, Sandy [a dog]. We go exploring, fishing, wading, or just walking. Sandy has no regulations binding him, so he goes swimming at will, a will stimulated by a stick tossed out.

Sunday, June 16, 6:15 p.m.
Boy, the food today. Let it not be said that the CCC boy never goes hungry, on Sunday anyhow. Two rolls, two slices of bread and butter, cereal, half-pint of milk and coffee for breakfast—and an orange. At noon, meat, potatoes, cake, coffee, tomatoes, bread and butter, and for supper, tomatoes, cottage cheese, bread and butter with sliced ham or American cheese for sandwiches. Plenty of strawberries for dessert and orange aid.

Monday, June 17, 3:00 p.m.
There's to be a lecture on resuscitation tonight, as a preliminary to bathing. I suppose there will be a series of lectures, exams, and diplomas issued with all the trimmings, then after that they get a fleet of rowboats, a dozen life savers, couple of life guards, fence in a few square feet, build a raft, then they might let us go in for a few minutes each day, provided we don't go in water over our knees.

Sunday, July 21, 2:00 p.m.

We finished the big [swimming] tests yesterday morning. I got through them all but the double wrist grip, which I had to do twice. Got the Senior but not the Examiner's rating.

Monday, July 22, 2:00 p.m.

Alf and I took the boys out swimming yesterday with a greatly changed viewpoint. Buddy system. I may be able to get a swimming class going pretty soon.

Took in the camp movie last night, Jimmy Durante and Lee Tracy in *Carnival*.

Friday, August 16, 11:00 p.m.

Big day today, 3655 reverted back to 640 and 30 rookies dropped in from Illinois.

Sunday, August 18

Had a little swimming but raining steady now. The rookies have their clothes now so they don't look so "hicky."

Tuesday, August 20, 1:30 p.m.

Been raining all morning so the boys went out at twelve and worked until 4:30. We had about twenty men practicing the [swimming] test yesterday afternoon. Some of them will pass without any trouble, but a lot of them have trouble with floating.

Saturday, September 14, 10:30 p.m.

I went up to the school this morning and met Kendrigan and Brownell, but said nothing to them. [I met] with the Dean. Everything seemed satisfactory. I got plenty of encouragement. Interviewed Brownell last, which was accomplished gracefully enough. He said they'd be proud to claim me as an alumnus.

Now to get back to camp tomorrow to get ye olde discharge.

Got a lot of enthusiastic plans now that I am practically a college boy again. Wish the next few days were over.

Tuesday, September 17, 10:30 p.m.
I escaped with winter underwear, entire new khaki outfit, new shoes, overcoat (a dandy) and a couple of odds and ends. [I] had a funny feeling in my stomach saying goodbye to some of the fellows. Well tomorrow, I start another life.

Thursday, September 26, 12:30 p.m.
Discharge paper neatly tucked away in a box of souvenirs. Check for three bucks with it.

J. Allen Spoolman graduated from Northland College in 1937 with a degree in English. While he was there, he enjoyed singing in the choir, acting in a play, playing basketball, and dating. In 1938, he worked for a brief time at CCC Camp Delta as a music instructor. When World War II broke out, he enlisted in the Merchant Marine. Upon returning from the war, he attended Western Illinois State University where he earned a bachelor of engineering degree and an Illinois State High School Teaching Certificate in 1946. He taught art for one year (1946–1947) at a junior high school in Galesburg, Illinois. As his nephew Scott Spoolman wrote, "He had a hard time sticking with anything. He never married. Wanderlust struck him. He worked on the ore boats on the Great Lakes, mostly as a cook. He eventually retired and lived with his brother in Ashland where he died in 1976."[1]

Part II

The CCC Camp

6

WISCONSIN CCC CAMPS

The first CCC camp in Wisconsin, Camp Brinks, was manned by CCC Company 640. It opened on May 4, 1933. The camp was built on the far western edge of the town of Washburn on the Ora Brinks home site. There CCC members planted jack pine trees, built roads, and helped with fire protection until 1941, when the camp closed.[1] By the end of 1933, fifty-eight CCC camps had sprung up in Wisconsin across the northern counties of the state, but also farther south in West Allis, Argyle, Lancaster, Darlington, and Evansville. More would open in the years that followed.[2]

On May 4, 1935, Wisconsin's quota of CCC camps nearly doubled, from fifty-five to ninety-five. The creation of more soil conservation camps precipitated the rise. An Ironwood, Michigan, newspaper in 1935 reported the following regarding the predicted upturn of CCC enrollees and camps in Wisconsin:

> In making the announcement today, Robert Fechner, director of emergency conservation work, said the number of men working on CCC projects in Wisconsin would be increased from 11,000 to approximately 21,000. The number of men from the state will be increased from 11,349 to 14,000. Thirty of the new camps will be in national and state forests, nine in state parks and one on a wildlife conservation project. . . . Altogether the state will have 70 camps devoted to forest improvement and protection work. Locations of soil conservation camps will be announced later, he said.[3]

It is estimated that between 1933 and 1942, the total number of CCC camps operating in Wisconsin ranged from 103 to 128.[4] The exact number of companies that went through these camps is difficult to determine because CCC companies tended to operate in one area with one designation, then move to another area with a different designation. What is well known, though, is that by 1942, when the CCC was officially dissolved, more than ninety-two thousand men had been put into service improving the state's natural resources as members of the CCC.[5]

Of the forty-five camps operating in Wisconsin in 1938, thirteen were devoted to soil conservation and were led by the federal Soil Conservation Service. These included camps at West Salem, Onalaska, Glen Haven, Nelson, Argyle, Platteville, and Coon Valley. Workers at these camps constructed terraces, worked on drainage control, and did some tree planting, including planting for windbreaks.

Additional camps were established in national forests with firefighting, tree planting, and other such activities the primary assignments. Initiatives at these camps, most of which were located in northern Wisconsin counties with camps at Florence, Drummond, and Three Lakes, were directed by representatives of the Forest Service.

Others were in state parks and forests, where recruits planted trees and constructed facilities. Finally, seven camps operated in Wisconsin state parks, where the CCC constructed buildings, built roads, and made other improvements.[6]

A winter view of Camp Beaver near Clam Lake. WHI IMAGE ID 53918

Camp Culture

While all CCC camps had similar characteristics each was also unique, due to its location. Some camps were close to villages, and others were quite isolated. Some enrollees primarily planted trees, and others built erosion control devices, constructed park buildings, and performed an array of other duties. And of course, enrollees and their supervisors made each camp unique, as young men from all parts of the country brought with them their nationalities, backgrounds, and experiences.

Camp Designations

Civilian Conservation Corps camps, organized as military companies with numerical designations, were later assigned letter designations based on their work assignments. Camps engaged in forestry work were assigned the letter *F*, while those working on soil conservation projects were assigned the letters *SCS*. Other lettered abbreviations included *NP* for CCC operations in national parks and *CP* for CCC camps in county parks. Many of the CCC camps in Wisconsin carried F or SCS designations.[7]

A group photo of enrollees at Camp Sheep Ranch near Phillips. COURTESY OF TERESE TROJAK

The CCC in the Chequamegon National Forest

The Chequamegon National Forest includes 858,400 acres in Ashland, Bayfield, Sawyer, Price, Taylor, and Vilas Counties in northern Wisconsin. At one time or another the following CCC camps operated in the Chequamegon National Forest in Wisconsin:

Camp Beaver, Clam Lake

Camp Brinks, Washburn

Camp Cable, Cable

Camp Chippewa River at Loretta, Loretta

Camp Clam Lake, Clam Lake

Camp Delta, Delta

Camp Drummond, Drummond

Camp Ghost Creek, Hayward

Camp Horseshoe, Moquah

Camp Jump River, Jump River

Camp Loretta, Loretta

Camp Mineral Lake, Marengo

Camp Mondeaux River, Westboro

Camp Moose River, Glidden

Camp Morse, Morse

Camp Perkinstown, Perkinstown

Camp Pigeon Lake, Drummond

Camp Riley Creek, Fifield

Camp Sawyer, Winter

Camp Sheep Ranch, Phillips

Camp Taylor Lake, Grandview[8]

Camp Riley Creek, Fifield

Camp Riley Creek in Fifield, Wisconsin, began to take in recruits on May 14, 1933, only ten days after the first CCC camp opened in Washburn, Wisconsin. Here is how one CCC historian recorded the event:

It was on May 11th, 1933, that a group of khaki clad young men stepped off the morning train at Fifield, WI, and were met by a Model T mail truck, which was to transport them to their new home, Camp Riley Creek. There was only room for a few on the truck so the remaining boys started walking the fifteen miles to the camp site. The truck continued making trips back and forth until the entire company had arrived safely at the destination.

There were no orderly rows of neat buildings to greet the eyes of the young pioneers, but only a stump covered clearing, a pile of tents, and plenty of tools to work with. Tents were set up and the camp was established. A small building belonging to the Forest Service was used as an office, and together with a warehouse, also owned by the Forest Service, were the only buildings on the site.[9]

The CCC campers did their work well. By 1940, Camp Riley Creek had a permanent set of buildings—several barracks, mess hall, camp canteen, and library. The canteen, run by a CCC enrollee, sold small but extremely desirable items such as candy, combs, pipes, and tobacco. The library was a quiet place for study and letter writing, and educational classes were offered in the evening.[10]

In 1940, army leadership at Camp Riley Creek included a Regular Army officer in charge, a second in command, a physician, an educational advisor, and a chaplain, all of whom were in charge when enrollees were in camp. When in the field, recruits were supervised by Forest Service personnel. Among the enrollees, ten were leaders and sixteen were assistant leaders.[11]

Camp Mondeaux River, Westboro

On June 11, 1933, a small number of CCC enrollees in Company 1603 left Fort Sheridan, Illinois, bound for Westboro, Wisconsin. It was their assignment to establish a camp in the Chequamegon National Forest near the Mondeaux River. Nine days later, the main body of the company left Fort Sheridan for Westboro. All were disappointed to see a campsite burned over and filled with stumps. Still, the men got to work. By 1935, the camp, now much more than a stump-covered field, had expanded its numbers and split, the new group forming Camp Jump River located nine miles from the present site.

Like other CCC recruits across the United States, the boys at Camp Mondeaux River made sport their pastime. Many played basketball and boxed competitively. Where they excelled, however, was on the baseball diamond. Their team won the Taylor County Baseball League in 1935, going undefeated that season.[12]

Camp Beaver, Clam Lake

CCC Company 1604 began its work at Camp Beaver, near Clam Lake in the Chequamegon National Forest, on June 21, 1933. During the winter of 1933–1934, members of the CCC roughed it in tents. Barracks construction began in the spring.

Many CCC recruits trained at Fort Sheridan in Illinois before they were sent to camps in Wisconsin. This photo shows CCC Company 1604 marching at the fort. WHI IMAGE ID 53910

A BIG BANG

Raymond S. Subczak served in the CCC at Camp Beaver. Raymond and his fellow enrollees worked on trails and other forestry projects and helped improve the camp as it moved from tents to wooden barracks. During the improvement process, a large tree stump needed removal. The company's army captain asked if any of the boys had experience using dynamite. Raymond raised his hand.

"Where did you use dynamite?" the captain asked.

"At home on the farm," Raymond responded.

Raymond was put in charge of removing the gigantic stump. He selected a few of his fellow CCC members to help him dig a big hole under the stump. The captain gave him the keys to the dynamite shed and told Raymond to find what he needed. Looking at the stump, Raymond at first thought a half-stick of dynamite would do the job. But to make sure, he decided to use a whole stick. He cleared the area of all the men and lit the fuse, then ran away to a safe distance. Unfortunately, the stump was within fifty feet of the camp's new dining hall. The blasted stump shot up into the air, moving higher and higher, and then it came down—through the roof of the dining hall.

No one was hurt, but the captain came charging out of his office, saw the hole in the roof, and ordered Raymond front and center. He grabbed the keys from Raymond and shouted, "I don't want you near dynamite shed ever again!"

For the rest of his tour at Camp Beaver, Raymond drove the camp truck, responsible only for hauling men from the camp to their worksites.[14]

The men of Camp Beaver stayed busy through the year. In the fall, they carved out a rustic football field near their new barracks. They played football with other CCC camps in the Chequamegon National Forest, winning the district championship.[13]

Company 1604 spent two years at Clam Lake before moving to Richland Center in 1935, where they did soil conservation activities. The company moved again when their work at Richland Center was through, this time to Gays Mills.

The CCC in the Nicolet National Forest

The Nicolet National Forest is in northeastern Wisconsin and includes parts of Forest, Oconto, Florence, Vilas, Langlade, and Oneida Counties. It covers 664,822 acres. When CCC numbers were at their peaks, twenty-three camps were stationed in the Nicolet National Forest. The first was Nine Mile Camp, established in the spring of 1933.[15]

At one time or another, the following CCC camps operated in the Nicolet National Forest in Wisconsin:

Camp Alvin, Alvin

Camp Bear Paw, Mountain

Camp Blackwell, Laona

Camp Boot Lake, Townsend

Camp Cavour, Laona

Camp Double Bend, Newald

Camp Dream, Florence

Camp Himley Lake, Wabeno

Camp Lakewood, Lakewood

Camp Lily Pad, Phelps

Camp Long Lake, Long Lake

Camp Mountain, Mountain

Camp Newald, Newald

Camp Nine Mile, Eagle River

Camp Phelps, Phelps

Camp Pine River, Three Lakes

Camp Rainbow, Florence

Camp Scott Lake, Three Lakes

Camp Section Eleven, Townsend

Camp Thunder River, Lakewood

Camp Trump Lake, Wabeno

Camp Virgin Lake, Three Lakes

Camp Wolf River, Lakewood [16]

Camp Smith Lake, Seeley

It was from Fort Sheridan that the two hundred young men from Wisconsin in CCC Company 647 left Illinois for the Northwoods in early May 1933. When they reached their destination, they made a temporary camp near Seeley, Wisconsin, near the Nicolet National Forest. Here campers built roads and undertook Forest Service projects, all while constructing a permanent home about five miles east of Seeley on the shores of Smith Lake. The campers finished their work in the fall and moved into their permanent quarters on October 15. Interestingly, the CCC campers at Smith Lake built themselves something of a novelty, a two-story barracks equipped with ropes hanging from the upstairs windows to serve as fire escapes.

Their ingenious design came in handy. In January 1935, a defective chimney caused a fire that destroyed five buildings in camp, including three of the two-story barracks. The rope fire escapes no doubt saved lives. Later that year the camp pump house caught fire, though most of the building was saved.

With a nod toward the history of fire at Camp Smith Lake, camp management set up a commemorative fire drill in January 1937. It didn't go as planned, though not in the way one might expect—nobody could get a fire started.

Camp Boot Lake, Townsend

Two CCC companies kept camp together at Camp Boot Lake near Townsend. Company 2619 staked first claim to the ground in September 1934. Company 3642 arrived afterward in June 1935. Anthony A. LaBrosse enlisted in the CCC in late 1934 at the age of seventeen and was assigned to Company 2619. Work at Boot Lake was tedious, consisting mostly of removing dead and dying trees in the forest and planting new ones in their place. Richard LaBrosse, Anthony's son, writes that "when somebody got caught doing something wrong, they were put on the firewood cutting crew.

Each barracks was heated with wood fires in old 55 steel barrels, with three stoves per barracks."[17]

WISCONSIN CCC VETERANS CAMPS

With Executive Order 6129, dated May 11, 1933, President Roosevelt authorized the immediate enrollment of twenty-five thousand veterans of the Spanish-American War and World War I in the CCC. There were no age or marital restrictions, though veterans who signed up needed to be unemployed. These men were housed in camps separate from younger enrollees and carried out duties suited to their age and physical condition.[18] Veterans were admitted to the CCC on a quota system. More populated states were allowed to send more veterans to the CCC.

Camp Evansville, Evansville

Company V-1680, a company of veterans established on July 25, 1934, was located at the former Rock County Fairgrounds south of Evansville. Most of the veterans in the company had served in Wisconsin's Thirty-Second Division; the oldest in the group was fifty-five. About 80 percent of the men were married with families. Historian Ruth Ann Montgomery described the company's arrival in this way: "Company 1680 arrived by train from Fort Sheridan on July 26, 1933, and marched four abreast from the railroad station to the fairgrounds. Headed by Major Joseph L. Phillips, an army cavalry officer, the men set up tents that would sleep 24 campers each."[19]

The men made the company headquarters, storerooms, and dispensary under the old fairgrounds grandstand. They repaired the fine arts building so it could be used as a mess hall. The city of Evansville pitched in by extending electricity and city water to the fairgrounds so that all the buildings and the newly erected tents had electricity. Veterans here spent their time building a new gravel road to the camp and working with area farmers on soil conservation projects, such as building small dams on nearby farms to help prevent erosion.

The camp did not have permanent barracks and was therefore not suitable winter quarters. As a result, in mid-October, officials at Camp

Evansville, as it was fondly known in the area, received word that they would be moving to Glenn, Illinois, where the men would be put to work in a park along the Mississippi River. Montgomery writes of their departure: "The CCC's left Evansville in December. The local residents watched as they paraded to the depot led by the Evansville city band. Though the Evansville people hoped they would return the following year, the city of Edgerton had made preparations for a camp and the next CCC to come to this area was sent to that city. The purchase of perishable provisions at local stores and the work they performed on local farms was valuable to the Evansville economy."[20]

Camp Darlington, Darlington

The 186 World War I veterans of CCC Company V-1676 made ready for service at Camp Custer in Michigan from July 1 to July 16, 1933. From Camp Custer the company traveled to Camp Darlington in Wisconsin.

Men of the company were at first under the direction of the Flood Control Administration. This agency later would be absorbed by the newly formed Soil Conservation Service. Work at Camp Darlington consisted of building dams and other structures to prevent soil erosion and flooding. The men did their work with distinction, setting a record for laying the greatest amount of concrete, measured in yardage, of any CCC camp in Wisconsin. In addition to their flood control and soil conservation efforts, Camp Darlington men did a considerable amount of stream and river improvement.[21]

7

Around a CCC Camp

A Typical CCC Camp

Civilian Conservation Corps camps resembled, in layout more than architecture, the small towns found throughout America in the 1930s and early 1940s. Places for dining, sleeping, and recreation, along with work-related structures, were near each other and sometimes overlapped. At first, camps were made from permanent structures built by local builders with occasional help from enrollees. When the CCC left a camp,

The grounds of Camp Rib Mountain in 1940. COURTESY OF JEANNE EVERT

the facilities that remained were usually turned over to the community. Portable equipment was salvaged whenever possible.

Things changed in 1936. From that year onward, CCC camps were made of portable structures built from a precut standard design—some of the first portable buildings constructed in the nation. A camp plan become standardized in 1936 as well, requiring each camp to have four barracks, one mess hall, one classroom building, one latrine, bath houses, twelve structures to house officers, and other necessary buildings to support the operation. How planners arranged their camps varied widely and was often determined by topography, proximity to water, and regional climate.[1]

Where a CCC camp was located was foremost a matter of practicality. The camp had to be near sources of food (a town not too far away) and water. Camps also needed to be near worksites—a national forest, state or national park, or a hilly region when soil conservation was needed. In some cases, camps were built near a town or city if the assignment was to work on an urban project.

MOBILITY OF COMPANIES

How long a CCC company stayed in one place varied. Some CCC companies spent several years at the same site. Others kept camp at a site for a relatively short time before completing their assignments and moving on. The history of Company 1604 provides a good example of CCC company mobility. Beginning on May 30, 1933, enrollees in the company underwent several weeks of physical training at Fort Sheridan, Illinois. From there the company shipped out for Clam Lake, Wisconsin. On June 21, they established Camp Beaver in the Chequamegon National Forest, where the Forest Service supervised their work.

Nearly two years later, on May 7, 1935, Company 1604 left Clam Lake and moved to Richland Center, Wisconsin. They established Camp Richland Center and took up erosion control work, serving with Soil Conservation Service employees who provided technical assistance. Five soil technicians assigned to the camp contacted farmers within a fifteen-mile radius, offering them a five-year plan for establishing contour strips, cropland rotation, and woodland management. The CCC boys would provide the manpower and materials.

It wasn't long before Company 1604 picked up stakes again, this time during the fall of 1935. The company moved thirty-two miles to a camp-site two miles north of Gays Mills in Crawford County. The citizens of Richland County protested their leaving and hoped the company would return in 1936. But it did not happen. Still working on soil conservation, the company remained at Gays Mills until 1942.[2]

CCC Company 658 also did its share of moving around Wisconsin. Like Company 1604, it was organized at Fort Sheridan on May 27, 1933. On June 19, enrollees traveled by rail to a campsite established two miles east of Townsend, Wisconsin, at the site of an old logging camp called Section Eleven. Hence, for two years the company was known as Section Eleven. On December 6, 1933, the entire contingent transferred to a new site near Three Lakes, Wisconsin. Company 658 planted thousands of trees on the cutover land. They also surveyed fields and streams and did roadside cleanup.

On June 11, 1935, the company moved once more, this time headed for Irving, Wisconsin, near Black River Falls. Company 658 was to make the switch from forestry to soil conservation. At Camp Irving, as the new camp was called, the CCC built thirteen soil conservation dams and eight miles of field terraces, fenced out woodlots, and planted sixty-five acres of trees, all during the summer and fall of 1935. On October 8, 1935, the company moved from its tent camp into portable buildings, which had just been finished. During the winter, the CCC worked on a timber and rock crib on the Black River to prevent flooding in the town of North Bend. Corps members also quarried and crushed limestone during the winter months, with nearly 1,300 tons of lime delivered to farmer cooperators.[3]

Some companies did their jobs in more than one state. Company 606 began work in Oregon, then moved to California. In 1934, the company transferred to Idaho, then returned to California, then went back to Idaho again. As well traveled as any company in the CCC, Company 606 returned to Fort Sheridan on October 1935 for reassignment. On November 7, 1935, the company found itself at Camp Rainbow near Florence, Wisconsin. By the time the company reached Wisconsin, it had operated in five states with eleven commanding officers.[4]

The record for moves, though, might belong to Company 604, which found its way to the Laona area in November 1935. After organizing in 1933, the company found itself at Camp Peterson in Guler, Washington,

MEMORIES OF THE CAMP CANTEEN
AND MESS HALL

Guy Christenson served at Camp Connors Lake near Phillips, Wisconsin. He described his memories of the canteen and mess hall in this way:

The canteen was a neat long building housing tables, complete with pen and paper for writing home, and some books and newspapers donated by nearby town people. There were the usual candy and cigarettes for sale, as well as shaving supplies. There was always some 3.2 beer (low alcoholic), soda pop and snacks available. We had a ping pong table and that was the scene of many an all-night game between some of the guys, who were betting on the outcome.

The mess hall was a long building with two rows of tables lining the sidewalls. We usually kept the tables set up for the next meal. There were three pot-bellied barrel stoves, all shined up with stove black to keep us warm. The winter of 1934 was a pretty cold winter as I recall. There was a fireman who worked all night keeping up all the fires. Those stoves needing filling about every two hours. There were ceiling lights hanging down the middle of the room, with black cone-shaped shades. There was a piano at one end of the mess hall and we had a lot of sing alongs. We had the best piano player you ever heard, a guy by the name of Steen from Eau Claire, Wisconsin. When Steen first signed on, he was a potato peeler. He could out peel every guy in camp with those fingers. He could play beautiful classical music, as well as popular tunes. We started a barbershop quartet and ended up with a pretty good glee club.[5]

in October. In mid-October, it was reassigned to Vancouver Barracks in Washington. There the company remained for all of four days (it picked up a new contingent of men) before heading to Camp Rock Creek in California, later named Camp Valyermo. In April 1934, the company traveled to Lower Beaver Camp, Idaho. From there it was back to Camp Valyermo in October 1934. The following May, the company made its way to Lowell, Idaho. By late summer 1935, Company 604 had partially disbanded with only a clerk, senior foreman, supply man, first aid man, mess steward, three cooks, and a baker in its ranks. The remainder of the company was either transferred out or discharged. What was left of Company 604 eventually reached Fort Sheridan, Illinois, and remained there for sixteen days while men from Illinois and Michigan filled its many vacancies. On November 6, 1935, Company 604 embarked from Fort Sheridan bound for Camp Blackwell in Laona. There they remained for nineteen months.

Camp Barracks

Camp barracks were at first nothing more than six-man army tents left over from World War I. Tents were heated with a woodstove, but they did not do much to keep out the cold in the wilds of northern Wisconsin and other cold-weather regions. A few unlucky CCC recruits suffered through their first CCC winters in these drafty shelters. When spring came, the army, working with local carpenters, constructed wooden barracks to house forty to fifty men at CCC camps around the United States. Barracks were typically one hundred feet long by twenty-four feet wide. In addition to his bunk, each man had a narrow place to hang his clothes and

A look inside the barracks at Camp Petenwell near Necedah. WHI IMAGE ID 109121

a footlocker on the floor in front of his bed. As many as three woodstoves constructed from steel barrels heated the barracks in cold climates.

Lawrence Kant worked at Camp Sailor Lake and recalled when the first barracks were constructed there. Kant's company was organized on June 20, 1933, so he and his fellow corps members lived in tents throughout the summer and fall of that year. As Kant recalled:

> Erection of the barracks began on October 14th . . . all buildings were closed in by October 28 . . . on November 13, orders came from President Roosevelt to allow the use of the incompleted barracks to reduce illness and so 206 men crowded into the three of the six barracks under construction. It was crowded for the two weeks required to make the remaining barracks livable and then each barrack was utilized by 32 men.
>
> Each barrack was issued 14 candles a week. Electric wires were strung to the barracks on November 22, but the electric generator did not come until January 4, 1934. The D. C. output would cause the lights to flicker more than the candles and reading was difficult, indeed.
>
> It wasn't exactly summer in those barracks. Each barrack had three wood burning stoves, with long pipes leading through the ceiling. The stove doors opened from the front so the firepot could handle 18" wood, which was hauled into the barracks after each day's work period. On a real cold night, those stovepipes would get red hot.
>
> The barracks cost $4,000.00 each. A lumberman from Phillips donated $12,000.00 toward building the barracks.[6]

Side Camps

"Side" camps were often established for short periods of time to complete a specific task. Enrollees at side camps were usually few in number and under the supervision of a junior army officer and a work project foreman. Working in a side camp also meant a return to tent camping. Guy Christianson remembered a side camp where he worked when he was stationed at Camp Connors Lake: "In the summer of 1935, twelve of us were sent to the small logging community of Winter, Wisconsin. We set up our camp in old Army tents and began to build a ranger station."[7] The twelve men at the Winter side camp worked with a local stone mason. He had a machine that made the cement blocks used to construct the building.

Camp Communication

A Signal and Ordinance Department was organized at the Sparta CCC District in the fall of 1935 to keep lines of communication open between the outside world and camps in the region. The ordinance part of the department's responsibility was relatively simple—providing each camp with a .45 caliber Colt automatic pistol to protect the company payroll. The signal part was a bit more complicated.

Each company was given a radio broadcast receiver. In their spare time, enrollees were allowed to use the radio for entertainment. In early 1936, the headquarters at Sparta received four 28-watt radio transmitters for the purpose of developing a radio network among the CCC companies in the district. The transmitters were located at Sparta, Blackwell, Mercer, and Cable. Another transmitter was eventually kept at Camp Crivitz. When Camp Crivitz closed, the transmitter was moved to Camp Peninsular in Door County. In May 1937, another radio station came on the air broadcasting from Camp Pattison, near Superior, which also served the National Park Service as well as the army. At the time, more than one thousand radio messages a month were handled by these radio stations.[8]

Camp Health

In the Sparta District of the CCC, each camp had one surgeon in residence at all times. He was to keep the men well. To do so, the surgeon supervised camp sanitation and cared for the ill and injured.

Enrollees attended weekly lectures given by the camp surgeon in which he gave overviews of disease and accident prevention. The surgeon also lectured on Red Cross First Aid and emphasized the importance of practicing good sanitation and personal hygiene. Cooks and food handlers were given weekly physical examinations by the surgeon to keep contagious diseases out of camp. The surgeon also checked every recruit during compulsory monthly physical examinations, and with the cooperation of the Wisconsin State Board of Health, every man in the CCC was tested for tuberculosis. When a member of the CCC became seriously ill or was badly injured, he was transported to a nearby hospital for treatment.[9]

8

EVERYDAY LIFE IN A CCC CAMP

Most CCC recruits entered a world about which they knew very little when they arrived at camp for the first time. Life in a rustic setting tucked deep in a national forest, for instance, was not the same as living in Milwaukee, Chicago, or Detroit, big cities from which the CCC drew many of its numbers. Many recruits had never been away from home, and a great many more had never lived a day in isolated conditions surrounded by a couple hundred young men whom they had never met. So too were the disciplinary standards of the US Army a shock, as army officers made it clear from the start that enrollees had not signed up for a camping trip in the woods but were expected to work hard and get results.

It is somewhat surprising, then, that only a small number "went over the hill." Those who did were recruits who could not adjust to life in camp and became deserters with dishonorable discharges. For the vast majority of the boys, however, being in the CCC meant having a paying job—something they could get almost nowhere else. That fact alone kept them in camp. Besides employment, recruits got free meals, free housing, and free clothing. They also had a golden opportunity before them to pick up vocational skills and participate in educational activities that inspired confidence, expanded their worldview, and prepared them for a richer future.

An enrollee at Camp Devil's Lake near Baraboo. WHI IMAGE ID 84588

The Daily Routine

David S. Rouse was with the CCC at Camp Devil's Lake. He recalled a typical day at camp like this:

> 6:00 a.m.: The bugle sounded reveille. Fifteen minutes later an army sergeant stormed into the bunkhouse. If a recruit was not up, his bunk was tipped, spilling him on the floor.

> 6:30 a.m.: Report to the parade grounds for fifteen minutes of calisthenics and then dismissal for breakfast. After breakfast, policing the grounds, and making bunks. The blanket on a bunk had to be tight enough so when a nickel was dropped on it the nickel would bounce.

> 7:45 a.m.: Join pre-assigned work groups, which varied depending on the work to be done. Eight men for fencing. Twelve men for landscaping. Sixteen men for planting trees. A leader accompanied each group.

12:00 p.m.: An hour for lunch, which consisted of sandwiches, cake or cookies, and a beverage. The camp cook sent lunches along with each work detail.

4:00 p.m.: Work stopped and the men returned to camp where they washed up, changed to their olive drab uniforms and reported to the parade ground for lowering the flag.

5:30 p.m.: Supper. After supper enrollees wrote letters, visited the camp recreation building, read books from the camp library, or stopped by the camp's canteen for a snack. (Candy bars were five cents as was a bottle of Pepsi-Cola.)

10:00 p.m.: Lights out.

10:15 p.m.: The camp bugler played taps.[1]

Rudy Kubik, a member of Camp Moose River near Glidden, Wisconsin, remembered the regular camp routine when he was stationed there in 1934:

We worked five days a week. The bugle sounded at 6:00 a.m. for wakeup call and we washed, dressed, and tidied up our bed and area for inspection. Then at 7:00 a.m. we had revelry and stood in line for the flag raising; then we had breakfast. After breakfast, we were assigned to our truck to be transported to a wooded area that had a fire loss. We cut down many tall cedar trees, which were then used for telephone poles. In the winter months, we had four feet of snow and had to form a four-man abreast line to trample and stomp the snow down so the horses could snake the poles out to the road.[2]

Bill Stark joined the CCC in 1939 and was stationed at Camp Riley Creek, near Fifield, Wisconsin. He recalled that in his first days at camp, he and his fellow campers were busy harvesting timber to construct camp facilities. They worked with axes and two-man saws. Around four o'clock, they returned to camp hungry for supper, which was served at six o'clock. Stark recalled that he was always hungry and sometimes volunteered for dishwashing duty so he could spend time in the kitchen and help himself to cookies. Stark also remembered Saturday mornings, when recruits had to drill, march, stand in parade formation, and pass inspection in military dress. The military men in camp also judged how CCC members kept their quarters. The bunkhouses where enrollees lived were subject to daily inspections. If the bunkhouse passed inspection, Stark recalled, the military inspector posted a big OKAY sign on the door. Of course, young men will be young men. Stark remembered that to break the daily grind, recruits would have a little fun of their own making. One trick was to hang upside down from a bar, with only your toes for support. Another was to toss a fellow CCC enrollee in the air with a blanket.[3]

Richard Schoenborn of Phillips joined the CCC in 1938 and was also assigned to Camp Riley Creek. Schoenborn also remembered military-style inspection, noting that "every Saturday we had a half day of inspection. We had to have a 'spit and polish' shine on our shoes, our shirts creased just so and our living quarters spotless or else we pulled extra duty."[4] Schoenborn recalled that if they didn't pass inspection, recruits would be assigned extra duties during what were supposed to be leisure hours. The men at Camp Riley Creek were free of work assignments from Saturday afternoon through Sunday, which was true of most if not all the CCC camps. For an enrollee to leave camp, though, he needed a pass. Passes were given so camp administration knew exactly how many men were

A trunk like this one held an enrollee's clothes and personal items. COURTESY OF STEVE APPS. PHOTO USED WITH PERMISSION FROM THE PIONEER PARK HISTORICAL COMPLEX.

Cooks stand behind their work at Camp Sheep Ranch. COURTESY OF TERESE TROJAK

in camp at any one time. Not every CCC member could leave at the same time, as some men were always needed in camp to react in the event of an emergency, such as a forest fire.[5]

KITCHEN PATROL (KP)

Enrollees helped with KP, or kitchen patrol, as the army named it. KP duty entailed such tasks as peeling potatoes, helping the head cook with baking, washing dishes, or doing whatever else needed to be done. Guy Christianson was in Company 1610 at Camp Connors Lake near Phillips, Wisconsin. Christenson joined the CCC in the spring of 1934 when he was twenty years old. He recalled the menu from Christmas Day that year, which he helped prepare.

> There were three cooks per shift, and two shifts, so a total of six cooks and one baker. On Christmas we all pitched in, even our mess sergeant. We started the feast with oyster stew. Now that was a rare delicacy for the Depression era, and for the Northwoods. We had roast goose with oyster and sage dressing, mashed white potatoes and baked sweet potatoes with brown pan gravy. There was also fresh

lettuce salad, celery sticks, olives, raisin bread, sweet and sour pickles, cranberry relish, fruit salad, mincemeat pie, cookies, nuts and candies. I know there were a lot of folks that weren't eating that well on Christmas day, 1934. Eating at our camp that day were three lieutenants, an educational advisor, a superintendent, a head foreman, a surveyor, a mechanic, 13 leaders, 21 assistant leaders and 224 enrollees. That's a lot of oyster stew.[6]

J. Allen Spoolman kept a detailed journal of his time at Camp Pigeon Lake near Drummond, Wisconsin. Here is what he wrote about KP:

Monday, November 19, 1934, 8:30 p.m.
Thirteen hours of work today, from five to eight. Boy, what a helluva job. How anybody free white and twenty-one would voluntarily to go in for a job like that is more than I can see. Potatoes, I peeled them until my fingers were numb and serving almost drove me nuts. Dishes sticking out from all sides and me never remembering where the dishes belonged after I got them filled. It's the monotony that gets me—doing the same things over and over again with nothing to show for it. Wash 250 plates, cups, bowls, platters, eight hundred knives forks and spoons. Set thirty-five tables, then start over and do it again—three times. I'll be one happy youth when the next four days are over. Saturday and Sunday will be a cinch with only thirty or forty men in camp.
    Miserable weather to work in the field—that's the only consolation.

Tuesday, November 20, 9:00 p.m.
Well, two more days down on the KP job. Today didn't even seem to go so bad. But tomorrow, Oh, Mamma. Tony and I wash dishes. Let's see, 220 plates, 220 cups, 220 bowls, 660 knives, forks and spoons, about 75 platters, 35 coffee pitchers. Oh, well, all of that times three—one long, greasy, backbreaking day.
    Rain all day. The crews didn't go out.[7]

C. C. C.
Thanksgiving 1935
Menu

English Celery   Olives

Roast Turkey

Sage Dressing   Giblet Gravy

Virginia Baked Ham

Mashed Potatoes   Sweet Potatoes

Creamed Peas   Shrimp Salad

Parker House Rolls

Mincemeat Pie   Pumpkin Pie

French Pastry

Mixed Fruit   Mixed Candy

Ice Cream   Coffee

Cigarettes   Cigars

This dinner was prepared under the supervision
of Alfred G. Rendler, Company Mess Steward.

During the Thanksgiving holiday, enrollees at Camp Nine Mile ate a special dinner in the mess hall. The Thanksgiving menu usually included the same foods that families around the country enjoyed at their tables. WHI IMAGE ID 105546

Mess halls, like the one shown here, needed to be large enough to seat more than two hundred hungry enrollees. COURTESY OF STEVE SYLVESTER

The Camp Cook

The old adage that "an army marches on its stomach" rang true in any CCC camp. Food was essential for a happy soldier and a happy camper. To make sure that happened, careful attention was paid to making sure the camp cook was first rate. Guy Christenson remembered many of the details of his assignment. Cooking was done on a woodstove, which had to be kept going all day. To make chili, for instance, cooks would put a kettle of kidney beans on the stove first thing in the morning and cook them for at least half a day. In the afternoon, cooks placed the cooked beans on the back of the stove to simmer. The following day, cooks started working on another kettle of kidney beans and when they were almost done, they added the first kettle of beans to the second kettle. Then they chopped beef and added that and all the other ingredients to the chili—making enough to feed more than two hundred men.

Christenson recalled that the head cook, a mess sergeant, was a stickler for clean white uniforms in the kitchen. There were no fancy washing machines. To get the job done, Christenson had a small wooden barrel next to his bunk. He used a metal cone to work his white uniforms up and down in the soapy water until they came clean.[8]

Camp Discipline

In a section of *Your CCC: A Handbook for Enrollees* titled "Toeing the Line," the CCC's approach to discipline was spelled out:

> Instead of ordinances and laws, CCC camps have "regulations," determined by those in charge of administering the CCC. . . . Discipline in the CCC involves such things as hours and manner of work, time of eating and hours for sleeping, leaving camp except at specified times and type of dress and personal conduct toward officials and toward other enrollees. . . . There are no jails or guard houses in the CCC. A breach of discipline does subject enrollees, however, to the performance of extra duty, deductions from monthly pay allowance, or in extreme instances, to discharge from the corps. In cases where physical restraint is necessary, offenders are turned over to civil authorities.[9]

Medical Service

As Ray Hoyt wrote in his early report on the CCC, "More than 'open spaces' and trees are needed to make the forests healthy places in which to reside, especially when one has to live in close contact with 200 or more other persons."[10] The healthy and restorative properties of the woods, waters, and fields would on their own not be enough to keep enrollees feeling their best. Thus, the army was well aware of the need to provide superior health services to CCC members. Preventing illness in the camps and treating those who were injured was of the utmost importance. Army officers in charge of the camps therefore paid special attention to the quality of the water. They also made sure that food was stored and prepared under sanitary conditions. CCC recruits were vaccinated against smallpox and inoculated against typhoid at intake camps prior to ever arriving for work. Personal hygiene, sanitation, and first aid were stressed by the army as matters that every CCC member needed to take very seriously. First aid instruction included what to do about snakebite and sunstroke and how to use a tourniquet to stop blood flow. Accident prevention was also high on the list of educational priorities to make sure the work in the woods, or wherever the young men were working, was as safe as possible.[11]

Accidents happened, though. They could not be avoided entirely when axes and saws and bulldozers and men came together in the woods. Spoolman lists in his journals some of the accidents and injuries that he suffered and those suffered by some of his unlucky fellow recruits:

Thursday, January 24, 1935, 9:30 p.m.
Tony broke his arm this morning cranking the "Cat." He isn't sitting in the usual poker game tonight.

Wednesday, January 30, 9:30 p.m.
Boy, did I almost get killed this morning. Eight inch popple came down right across my neck. It was falling slow, and just pushed my head down into the snow. There were three "hang-ups." I got out of the way of two but stood right in the path of the third.

Thursday, February 7, 9:30 p.m.
Slim and I got the job of smashing down brush today and I nearly smashed my left eye. A piece of brush smacked one lamp so hard I saw stars, and it sure gave me plenty of grief the rest of the day. I should have gotten quarters because of it, but Ted didn't say so.

Friday, February 8, 11:00 p.m.
Today was a bad day in the woods. Two of them carried out on stretchers and three or four other with minor cuts. I got a nice little slice above the knee. Nick Jelish got the bad one though—a wicked cut along the side of his knee. Must have been a bad one, because they had to carry him out. Then someone felled a tree on poor Banjo Eyes.

Sunday, May 26, 6:30 p.m.
Tragedy showed up yesterday for the first time for 640. Little Ed O'Brien drowned while swimming in the lake after dinner. Seems hard to believe, and hard to understand why there couldn't have been more help. There was no alarm spread at all. Pretty hard on Hank I'm afraid. They were pretty thick.[12]

9

EDUCATIONAL, RECREATIONAL, AND RELIGIOUS OPPORTUNITIES

EDUCATIONAL OPPORTUNITIES

The 1937 federal legislation that renewed CCC funding also mandated that CCC camps offer educational programs to enrollees. Prior to 1937, there had been no such mandate in place, but education was a priority in camps from their earliest days. In 1933, Clarence Marsh was named the first director of education in the CCC. He was appointed to organize and encourage educational activities at camps. By 1934, a formal educational program for CCC enrollees was in place. Director Robert Fechner was not keen on the idea, as he feared education might interfere with assigned work programs. His fear proved to be misplaced, however, as quite the opposite happened. Educational opportunities for enrollees became one of the most popular and beneficial aspects of the CCC endeavor, providing recruits with much needed work and life skills.

While the CCC was required to offer enrollees educational programs, attendance was voluntary. Recruits were given educational instruction during nonworking hours. Normal work hours were eight hours a day, five days a week—so enrollees had considerable free time to take up learning whatever interested them. Each military district had an education supervisor whose staff oversaw the education of CCC men in many academic areas. These included typing, reading and writing, first aid, citizenship, motor mechanics, radio, printing, woodworking, cabinet making, and metal and leather crafts. Of course, not all of these courses were available at every camp, though every camp did offer something in the way of education to those assigned there. Educational advisors, often unemployed teachers, men and women alike, reported to education supervisors. Every CCC camp had an educational advisor, and in some instances, he or she moved between camps if it was practical to do so. The importance of having a good educational advisor was critical. The effectiveness of a particular camp's educational program depended on the qualifications and skills of the educational advisor as well as on the cooperation he or she got from the camp commander.[1]

Educational advisors had a presence outside of class as well. CCC enrollees often saw in the educational advisor someone whom they could trust. As historian Robert J. Moore points out, "Oftentimes among enrollees, the education advisor was the most popular and trustworthy adult at the camp. . . . [T]he education advisor had no legal authority over the men. He did not wear a uniform and could not order the boys about or require them to attend class. . . . [M]any enrollees viewed educational advisors as confidants."[2]

Educational committees were formed in every CCC camp to plan and discuss the education of CCC recruits. Committee members included the company commander, camp superintendent, and educational advisor. The topics of discussion varied but included information regarding the previous training of enrollees, work projects planned with learning opportunities, necessary equipment for training, possible use of outside educational institutions to assist with training, and camp personnel available as instructors.[3]

From Washington, DC, the education arm of the Department of the Interior acted in an advisory capacity to the army. Interior officials suggested the following aims for the CCC educational programs:

1. To develop in each man his powers of self-expression, self-entertainment, and self-culture.

2. To develop pride and satisfaction in cooperative endeavor.

3. To develop as far as practicable, an understanding of the prevailing social and economic conditions, to the end that each man may cooperate intelligently in improving these conditions.

4. To preserve and strengthen good habits of health and mental development.

5. By such vocational training as feasible, but particularly by vocational counseling and adjustment activities, to assist each man to meet his employment problems when he leaves camp.

6. To develop an appreciation of nature and of country life.[4]

Educational facilities at camps generally included libraries, movie projectors, and classrooms equipped with blackboards and desks. There was no standard curriculum or standard method of instruction. Recruits studied what they wanted to study. The educational advisor's role was to talk with enrollees, discover and nurture their interests, then arrange to locate appropriate study materials for them.

Many educational advisors had to start with the basics. Jack Vincent served as an educational advisor at Camp Richland Center. Vincent claimed that, "My work was to teach over 150 boys how to read and write. They had to write a letter home and read a newspaper before they got the coveted reading and writing certificate. I also got 182 boys their high school diplomas."[5] Camp Richland Center, in addition to offering basic education and high school academic classes, provided classes in typing, truck driving, mechanics, bookkeeping, journalism, cooking, and baking.

Elsewhere, at the CCC camp in Devil's Lake State Park, popular courses were given in mechanical engineering, air conditioning, and vehicle maintenance. Popular informal classes offered were woodworking, public speaking, leatherwork, and photography.[6]

In the CCC camps in the Wisconsin Northwoods, CCC educational advisors often stressed the need for recruits to learn the practical and basic elements necessary to good forestry. Several of the practical skills CCC enrollees learned included "how to develop and maintain nurseries, how to plant seeds and seedlings, how to control pests and diseases of forested areas, how to prevent and fight forest fires, and how to use trees and forest products in landscaping."[7]

By 1940, CCC administration announced that educational programs had succeeded in teaching eighty thousand young men to read. As it turned out, three out of every one hundred CCC enrollees were functionally illiterate when they signed up for service in the CCC. To teach young men to read, the CCC devised special readers intended to be used by adults instead of children. The CCC was applauded by the *Springfield Daily News* of Springfield, Missouri, for its efforts. The paper believed it was a national embarrassment that eighty thousand young men could "slip through the educational system without getting the most elementary preparation for life—the ability to read and write. . . . Better late than never . . . the CCC thus sets another feather firmly in its cap."[8]

TEACHING AT A CCC CAMP

Teachers at CCC camps were both men and women, some of them just out of training programs. Lute Berkey shares his mother's memories as a CCC teacher:

My mother, Hazel Wagner, was hired to teach in a one-room school located at a remote CCC camp in Northern Wisconsin. Mom was young, cute, a petite 110 pounds and just out of school. Some of her pupils were as old as she. Many came from inner-city situations that were less than ideal. She had been educated to organize, manage, and teach in a one-room school. She could handle the varying ages and abilities. She could be a tough, no-nonsense, get the job done woman. Mom had grown up in Northern Wisconsin. She knew how to hunt, fish, snowshoe, and keep the woodstoves going.

She did recall one tense incident. It occurred with a rough looking fellow from Chicago. As she was bending over his work on his desk, she looked over his shoulder to see how he was doing. In the process she placed her hand on his shoulder only to encounter the feel of a shoulder holster. Looking below the shoulder, she saw the bulge of his gun. She hesitated just a moment, then gave his shoulder a pat and complimented him on his work. She moved on down the aisle. There were no negative incidences with him or any of the other CCC boys that she recalled.[9]

Camp Library

Each CCC camp included a well-stocked library of both fiction and non-fiction books. The selection of fiction regularly changed as new books became available. Many of the library's books were associated with the camp's educational programs, with a wide range of topics included. The library also contained weekly and monthly magazines as well as weekly and daily newspapers. The libraries were directed, maintained, and stocked as part of a CCC welfare program operated by the US Army.[10]

Offsite Educational Opportunities

Not only were educational activities offered at each CCC camp, but on occasion, CCC members were provided offsite educational opportunities as well. In 1941, Jerry Bayer was stationed at Camp Long Lake in northern Wisconsin. Jerry was not an especially strong young man. After his first week on a road crew, his superiors determined he was too frail for such strenuous work and put him on permanent KP in the mess hall. In July of the following year, Jerry was sent to the cooks and bakers school at the Sparta District CCC headquarters. After finishing cooking school, Jerry returned to the Long Lake camp as a cook.[11]

Education happened outside of camps in other ways too. The Sparta District CCC headquarters did what it could to help enrollees finish their elementary and high school educations. Headquarters made arrangements with the Wisconsin school districts in which camps were located so that the districts would recognize the educational work completed at the camps as contributing to the formal education of CCC recruits. Additionally, professionals such as bankers, carpenters, or plumbers were occasionally brought to camp as lecturers. Correspondence courses were also made available through the University of Wisconsin–Extension.[12]

Camp Organization for Technical Education

Technical training also occurred at CCC camps, overseen by the camp superintendent. Training programs varied among camps assigned to projects managed by the Forest Service, National Park Service, or Soil Conservation Service.

EDUCATIONAL OPPORTUNITIES

Camp Connors Lake in Phillips, Wisconsin, had an interesting and varied educational program open to recruits stationed there. Here are excerpts from an article in the camp newspaper describing the various courses and classes available.

The forestry class, under the able guidance of "Cap" W. W. Wisner and Mike O'Connell, seems to be the most popular class in the entire curriculum, and the consensus of opinion is that this is a surefire course. Last Thursday night, the camp superintendent, Mr. Ruhmer, spent the time explaining the ins and outs of fire tower work, showing the men the fire maps and explaining how they are used. This week a discussion of the telephone will be given the men. We are proud of our forestry course and we are thankful that the forestry personnel are cooperating in the fashion that they are.

The mechanical drawing course is another of the popular courses here, and we are lucky in having a former student of the University of Wisconsin, Mr. John Babback, to teach this class for us. Mr. Babback has had actual drafting experience, as he has worked for the Allis-Chalmers Corporation for some time. This course is patterned after the mechanical drafting classes of the Milwaukee Vocational School, and we are certain that the men are going to get a whole lot of good from participating in this work.

Of course the craft classes are drawing very heavily for almost everyone is interested in making things for themselves, and as we have leather craft, woodcarving and airplane modeling, the men have a variety of crafts to choose from.

The busiest place in camp is the quarters of the Educational Advisor and if you don't believe that this is a true statement just come around about six-thirty or seven any night that we are having classes.

The men are going to keep up the record of this company in the number of books read during the month; we have always had a record of 600 books read besides the magazines that are passed on from hand to hand. It is hoped that we will have a new shipment of books pretty soon.[13]

Professional technical advisors were paired with assistants drawn from the camp's staff. The *CCC Foremanship* handbook specified that "the superintendent will appoint the best qualified member of his staff as a training assistant. The training assistant will aid in planning the technical agency part of the program, keeping records, holding foreman conferences, and arranging for the instructing of foremen in training methods."[14] Nevertheless, administrators in Washington, DC, recognized that technical training in camps had its limitations. As the authors of the handbook admitted, "Much of the training can fit enrollees for labor jobs, fewer can be fitted for semi-skilled positions, and probably not more than ten percent can be trained to be skilled workmen."[15]

Of the many things CCC enrollees took away from their experiences in the CCC, the opportunity to advance their education proved to be one of the most valuable and enduring. The emphasis the CCC placed on general as well as vocational education—and the teaching approaches used in camps—served as a model that many adult education programs would follow long after the CCC shut down in 1942. The idea of starting with the learner's interests and building a series of educational opportunities around those interests was new at the time and in contrast with the approaches favored by formal secondary and postsecondary programs.

Recreational Opportunities

Life in a CCC camp was not all work and no play. On the contrary, recreation was an important part of the routine in many camps. Recruits did hard and often dangerous work, so it was necessary for them to spend time away from their labor to relax and recharge by themselves or with their fellow enrollees. As such, the roster of buildings in a CCC camp typically included a recreation hall. There, ping-pong, pool, and gymnastic equipment were generally available. In their downtime, men also did craft projects and acted in plays performed for the camp. Those who knew how to play an instrument played and sang with others when possible. Some camps had choirs.

THE FOUR-STEP METHOD

Beyond showing potential instructors how to break down a work project into specific skills to be learned, the foreman's handbook also suggested a specific instructional approach called the Four-Step Method. The Four-Step Method is described as follows:

Step I: Preparation. Devise a way so that the enrollee will be interested in wanting to learn the new skill. Ways to do this include asking the enrollee what he already knows about this skill, and showing him the importance of knowing it.

Step II: Presentation. Provide the enrollee with the information he needs to do this skill, and demonstrate how it is done. The extent to which this step is carried out depends on what the enrollee already knows about this skill and his performance level in carrying it out.

Step III: Application. The enrollee is given the opportunity to do the skill himself. If he has difficulty, the trainer will help him with further demonstration on how to do it. The trainer can ask questions to make sure the enrollee not only knows how to do the skill, but the reason for doing it in a particular way. For instance if the skill is planting trees, the trainer might ask, "Why is it necessary to firmly pack the roots around the tree when planting it?" (Correct answer is to remove any air pockets, which might invite mold to develop around the roots.)

Step IV: Test. This is to determine if the enrollee can perform the skill correctly without outside help. Fairly often, an enrollee will grasp how to do most of a skill correctly, but not all. Testing helps the trainer know what additional training might be necessary.

In summary, Step I motivates the enrollee to learn a skill, Step II shows him how, Step III allows him to try it, and Step IV determines how well the enrollee has learned the skill.[16]

CAMP ORCHESTRA

Camp Connors Lake organized a camp orchestra featuring guitar, drum, banjo, clarinet, and cornet players. Here is a story from *The Voice of 1610*, the camp's newspaper, describing the makeup of the orchestra.

> We have a new camp orchestra in the making now under the supervision of John Taplin and his assistant, Jerry Vujtech. So far there are 6 members in it, and we have hopes of getting a larger number later on. The men who now are in the orchestra are: John Taplin and his drum, Jerry Vujtech and his banjo, Wayne Miller and his clarinet, Red Dienburg and his guitar, Carl Gahj and his cornet and Robert Johnson and his cornet, Jews harp and roller mouth organ. Well, anyway, good luck to you fellows.[17]

Competitive Recreational Activities

Sports and athletics were another important dimension of camp life. The army provided athletic equipment to each camp and helped organize athletic programs.[18] Camps in the same district often competed against one another in sport, games, or theater. In Wisconsin, for example, Company 606, assigned to Camp Rainbow in Florence, distinguished itself in competition. The company won second place in the Sixth District competition

The CCC was never all work and no play. Enrollees at Camp Devil's Lake are shown here in trucks, perhaps on their way to town to have some fun. WHI IMAGE ID 84596

for one-act plays, second place in an indoor game tournament, fourth place in a two-man entry in the Sixth District swimming meet, and first place in diving during the years 1936 and 1937. Company 606 also competed in area baseball, softball, basketball, and track meets.[19]

Company 1602 out of Camp Petenwell, located four miles east of Necedah, had a thriving organized athletics program. It included boxing, basketball, track and field activities, plus volleyball and baseball. The Camp Petenwell teams, nicknamed the Panthers, competed with teams from Camp City Point in Wood County, along with others in the area.[20]

Guy Christenson recalled fondly the baseball team at Camp Connors Lake. They called their team the Wood Ticks. They were talented, as Christenson claimed: "We had the best darned team around. Some of the guys went on to play baseball in other bigger cities. . . . [W]e sure enjoyed our baseball team in those days."[21]

Horseshoes became a popular recreational activity at Devil's Lake State Park. In April of 1940, the CCC boys there organized a camp-wide horseshoe tournament. This was their way of celebrating the end of winter and the start of outdoor recreational activities. Horseshoes was popular at CCC

Enrollees swimming in Devil's Lake at Camp Devil's Lake. COURTESY OF JOHN DUCHAC

camps because it was easy to set up and games could be played during breaks and after the evening meal. The 1940 horseshoe tournament was one of the most popular competitions ever held at the camp, with more than one-third of camp enrollees signing up.[22]

The CCC boys of Company 3648 working in Fish Creek at Camp Peninsular played football against the local high school football team. Buck Eckert, a long-time Fish Creek resident, remembered that the CCC boys played in bare feet. He guessed their work boots were too heavy for football.[23]

GOING TO TOWN

The *Your CCC* enrollees' handbook included specific rules and regulations that CCC members who wished to leave camp had to follow. Enrollees wanting to get outside of camp had to obtain a pass from the commanding officer. A pass was given for a specific period of time, and if the enrollee did not return to camp after his leave time expired, he was AWOL (absent without leave). Being AWOL was a major offense that sometimes led to loss of pay, extra work, or even discharge from the CCC.[24]

For those enrollees living close to a village—which was the case for many—going to town on Saturday night was often the highlight of the week. One of the real treats was attending a dance. There recruits would have a chance to meet local girls. Kay Barnard, who grew up near Mondovi, Wisconsin, looked forward to the Saturday night dances when CCC boys from a camp near Gilmanton arrived in town. She wrote, "I enjoyed having the boys from the CCC camp come to the Saturday night dances. When they came, I got to dance every dance. To the best of my memory, the boys arrived in a truck—and departed in a truck. I don't remember any particular boy—but then I didn't go outside for a private conversation with any of them either. Some girls did go outside, but usually a relative followed rather quickly and returned with the girl."[25]

Therese Trojak grew up near Phillips and remembered Saturday evenings when men from the CCC came to town for dances held in the Legion Hall. Trojak said that "about five or six truck loads would ride by our home on Highway H, big trucks with five foot racks, with young men singing. They all enjoyed dancing and many romances bloomed at the gatherings. . . . The Legion Hall had a lovely hardwood floor and a large stage for bands."[26]

RELIGIOUS OPPORTUNITIES

Religious services were held in camps on Sundays. Attendance was not mandatory. David S. Rouse recalled that "every Sunday morning, religious services were performed at Camp Devil's Lake. . . . The camp had a small, simple chapel nestled in the woods back of the camp, where services were held. The right to worship was a respected part of CCC life."[27] The chaplain at Devil's Lake Camp counseled enrollees, visited those confined to the infirmary, and, on occasion, married a recruit who had asked one of the local girls to be his wife.

The Sparta District CCC headquarters provided one chaplain for every eight camps. Chaplains were assisted by contract and volunteer chaplains from nearby communities. Chaplains held Catholic and Protestant services at each camp at least once a week. They were also available to help enrollees with individual problems and concerns.

CHURCH AT CAMP SAILOR LAKE, FIFIELD

Lawrence Kant served in the CCC at Camp Sailor Lake near Fifield. He wrote the following about church services at his camp:

> The mess hall was also used as a recreation hall and for a church. Camp Sailor Lake had a unique arrangement for their religious program. The Company Commander is of the Catholic faith and he rounds up all the Catholic boys and takes them to Park Falls with him to make sure they go to church. The Executive Officer is of the Protestant faith, and if there is anyone in camp at 10:30 on Sunday morning when the District Chaplain arrives they are sure to be in church.
>
> Those of the Catholic persuasion use an army truck to transport them to a city to attend a segregated church service, while many of the other denominations of the Protestant faith were desegregated by decree and thus required to attend integrated worship in the mess hall; a simple Gospel message by a piano pounding chaplain.

Kant was not pleased with the situation, believing the Catholics got preferential treatment. He wrote: "That situation still rankles."[28]

10

COMMUNITY RELATIONS

CCC camps and the communities they bordered enjoyed a mutually beneficial relationship, and it was not unusual for a community to do special things for a CCC man. David S. Rouse recalled when he and a friend were hitchhiking home to Milwaukee from Camp Devil's Lake where they were stationed. Rouse and his friend had a weekend pass but no money for public transportation. On a one-below-zero winter weekend, the young men got a ride as far as Sun Prairie. There was little traffic, however, and hopes of hitching a ride the rest of the way to Milwaukee were slim. Because it was nighttime and two young men were standing idly on a lonely street corner, the village constable appeared and asked David and his companion what they were doing. They explained their circumstance. The constable suggested they accompany him to the jail, where he allowed them to sleep in warm cells with the doors open. The following morning, he escorted the CCC enrollees across the street to a restaurant for a big breakfast. Hitching was easier in the morning, and soon David and his friend were in Milwaukee.[1]

In an effort to get ahead of problems that might come up when more than two hundred young men suddenly arrived on the outskirts of communities that were sometimes smaller than the camps, CCC administration made every effort to acquaint townspeople with the CCC and the work they were doing. Town leaders were invited to camp to eat meals with the officers and men. In turn, CCC boys were invited to dances in town. As relations improved, recruits were often invited to nearby homes for meals. Some were even allowed to escort daughters to movies. Camp basketball

SCHOOL BAND ENTERTAINED AT
CAMP SHEEP RANCH, PHILLIPS

Sometimes the officials at a CCC camp would invite outside groups to provide entertainment at the camp. Here is an example.

Mr. Dunn, the Educational Instructor of the Sheep Ranch CCC Camp, invited Mr. Parker and the Phillips High School Band to spend an afternoon with the camp boys. The band gathered at the High School to await the trucks, which were to transport them to the camp. . . . [W]e arrived at the Camp about three o'clock, and changed into our band uniforms.

All the CCC boys were then gathered into the Mess Hall. Mr. Dunn began the program with a little talk to the boys, which was followed by a selection by the Phillips High Band. . . . The band played the "The Bells of Saint Mary" while Mr. Dunn sang the words. The High School group was then entertained by the Camp Choir, and the Camp Orchestra. . . . After the program, some of the band members went up to the Recreation Hall where they divided their interests among pool, ping pong, and the punching bag. Other members made an inspection of the Camp. . . . About six o'clock, the Band was served a delicious lunch, after which it was taken home.[2]

and baseball teams played against local teams. Eventually, townspeople visited camps on Sundays, participating in the recreational activities such as musical shows and plays written by CCC recruits.[3]

A June 9, 1934, newspaper article included a CCC inspection report about an event held at Camp Mondeaux River near Westboro. The article included this information:

Peaceful solitude along the Mondeaux River was broken by the hilarity of a mammoth party tossed by CCC Company 1603, Westboro, Wisconsin. A great crowd of girls, chaperons, and other guests was estimated at approximately 600. The mess hall was decorated with green and yellow crepe and set by evergreen branches and trees. The orchestra—well known as the Vagabonds—was placed in a miniature grove of trees and did themselves proud. Ice cream and punch was served.

Distinguished guests of the evening included Mayor Luepke, Mayor of Medford; Major Rodriquez, District Commander, and the District Chaplain. Many officers and forestry men from other camps attended. Farmers and businessmen of the surrounding community were well represented.[4]

Winter, Wisconsin, was the closest town to Camp Connors Lake. As Guy Christenson recalled: "We spent most of our off hours either in Winter or out at one of the area bars/dance halls. Most of us didn't have much money in our pockets, so we didn't worry about being over served. The majority of the fellows liked to dance, and we'd all pile in the back of the camp pickup truck and be off to the nearest dance hall whenever we could get the free time. . . . [There were also] outdoor movies, every Wednesday night [in Winter]."[5]

The CCC boys living at Camp Blue Lake often spent time in Minocqua. There they took in a movie, watched a ballgame, shopped at a local store, or did some gambling at several local establishments. Recruits at Camp Blue Lake usually caught a CCC truck to town, which returned to pick them up at eleven o'clock at night. If they missed the truck, they had to walk back to camp—a distance of about nine miles.[6]

James Skarda, a CCC enrollee at Camp Viroqua near Viroqua, Wisconsin, remembered how he and a fellow enrollee played baseball one summer and fall with the Viroqua city team. "We got to know the community," Skarda said. But there were some unfortunate occurrences as well. Skarda

James Skarda served in the CCC at Camp Viroqua. COURTESY OF JAMES SKARDA

Baseball was a popular pastime in camps. Camp teams often competed with teams from neighboring camps. In this photo, James Skarda waits for a pitch. COURTESY OF JAMES SKARDA

recalled a Sunday when he and several of his fellow CCC recruits attended a Catholic mass in Viroqua. "While we were setting in the congregation, the priest in his sermon said, 'I tell you folks, do not permit your daughters to associate with CCC boys. They will rape your daughters and they are nothing but drinkers.' Here we were, sitting out there taking all this in. When the mass was over, I went up to the altar to meet the priest. I said to him, 'Father, there were three CCC boys here today. Let me tell you something. I've never had a beer in my life. I don't smoke and I don't even have a girlfriend. You offended us; I wanted you to know that.' He said nothing."[7]

For the most part, though, CCC camps lived amicably alongside their neighbors. Forward-thinking camp commanders helped ensure peaceful relations by taking a proactive approach. In late August 1935, for example, the commander of Camp Devil's Lake invited 150 Baraboo businessmen to visit the camp. They toured the buildings and learned about the projects the boys were working on and would work on. Their visit concluded with an evening meal at the mess hall.[8]

Search and Rescue Operations

Sometimes CCC recruits paid service to those around them by helping during an emergency. The following newspaper article illustrates another way that two CCC companies endeared themselves to local communities:

Rhinelander, January 26, 1938

An expectant mother was rushed six miles over snow-blocked highways to a hospital in Laona late yesterday by a rescue expedition of 80 CCC enrollees working with shovels, two snow plows and a tractor.

The woman, Mrs. Stella Simonis, gave birth to a son about 45 minutes after completion of the arduous journey from her home at Blackwell, hospital attendants reported. They said she and the baby were "fine."

CCC enrollees from Camps Blackwell and Cavour shoveled for hours to open a path when plows and tractor were unable to penetrate the heavy drifts. As they advanced, swirling snow drifted the highway shut 100 yards behind them. Physicians said the boys' efforts probably saved the lives of the mother and son.[9]

The CCC boys of Camp Blue Lake also pitched in when they were needed most. On more than one occasion, they were involved in search and rescue operations in the area. Camp Blue Lake recruits searched for and found a woman lost in the woods in 1933. The following year, they searched for a lost airplane, then found a man lost at Squaw Lake in 1936. That same year, they found two boys lost near Rhinelander and recovered the body of man who drowned in Little Arbor Vitae Lake.[10]

PART III

CCC WORK PROJECTS

11

Overview of Projects

Legislatively approved CCC work projects numbered as many as three hundred. The National Advisory Committee for the CCC, made up of representatives from the War Department, the Department of Agriculture, the Department of the Interior, and the Department of Labor, developed a broad sweep of work projects for CCC enrollees to complete. The Forest Service and the National Park Service had previously developed long-range plans for projects in national forests and parks and were thus almost immediately prepared to put CCC enrollees to work.[1] The projects conducted in a particular state varied according to need. Projects were approved that not only corrected a local environmental problem but also raised new facilities, especially at state and national parks. Additionally, it was important that approved projects offer CCC enrollees a chance to learn at least one new skill. The nationally approved projects fell into ten general categories:

1. Improvement of structures such as bridges, park buildings, and fire towers

2. Transportation including building of forest roads and trails

3. Control of erosion involving terracing and laying out fields for strip cropping

4. Flood control, which included ditching, river channel work, and dam building

5. Forest improvement such as tree planting and nursery development

6. Forest protection that included firefighting and insect and disease control

7. Outdoor recreation including developing public camping and picnic grounds and clearing of lake and pond sites

8. Range work to improve grazing situations in western states

9. Wildlife improvement including stream improvement, building fish hatcheries, and stocking fish

10. Miscellaneous, which included emergency work such as doing surveys and mosquito control[2]

CCC enrollees in Wisconsin carried out at least one project in every category except the eighth, range improvement. Wisconsin CCC camps were organized by specific work projects. Camps were assigned lettered designations that indicated the type of work recruits were carrying out. For instance, camps in Wisconsin were assigned the following letters:

C of E = State land (Corps of Engineers)

F = National forest

PE = Private land erosion

S = State forest

SCS = Soil conservation

SP = State park

Projects with different letter assignments were often near each other. As a result, many CCC recruits worked on more than one project designation. For example, from 1937 to 1941, a training school for state and federal forestry personnel from Midwestern states was located on what is now the site of Trees for Tomorrow, near Eagle River, Wisconsin. (Trees for Tomorrow, which started in 1944, is a private nonprofit natural resources school with a mission of offering information on proper natural resource and forest management approaches.) CCC enrollees constructed the training school's administration building and a dining hall. They also helped construct other buildings on what is now the Trees for Tomorrow campus.[3]

Many enrollees had spent little time in the woods before arriving in camp. Those new to the outdoors quickly learned their way around the forest, as they were often asked to do the type of work shown here, where young men are pulling cedar logs over the snow.
COURTESY OF STEVE SYLVESTER

The letters in the alphabet soup of work assignments were strung together to create an amazing story of industry and environmental renewal. By the end of 1937, Robert Fechner noted that the CCC had provided jobs for more than two million persons and brought an economic upturn to manufacturers and small businesses around the country. From coast to coast and beyond, the CCC carried out more than 150 major types of work under the general headings of forest protection, soil conservation, recreational development, aid to wildlife, flood control, and soil conservation.[4]

How the Work Was Organized

Men in the CCC worked in small crews supervised by a foreman employed by the government technical service active in camp. The foreman might be an employee of the Forest Service or the Soil Conservation Service depending on whether the camp was committed to forestry or soil conservation. Either way, the foreman often delegated some of his supervisory duties

A recruit pauses from his work with a jackhammer to have his picture taken. COURTESY OF JAMES SKARDA

to designated crew leaders, CCC members who had been promoted to a position of leadership beneath the foreman. In addition to positions of leadership, enrollees were eligible for appointment to specialized positions at the camp such as mess steward, cook, canteen steward, assistant educational advisor, or night watchman. Some men were assigned to work as truck and ambulance drivers, in clerical positions, or as auto mechanics.[5]

Above the foreman was the camp superintendent in charge of all the project work done in camp. The superintendent supervised not only the foremen but also the skilled laborers in camp employed by a government technical service such as the Forest Service or the Soil Conservation Service. The superintendent had the added responsibility of being in charge of recruits when they left camp to go to town or elsewhere. When enrollees were in camp, the army was in charge of their welfare. Regardless of who was in charge, recruits were expected to take and follow orders. Failure to do so was grounds for discharge from the CCC.

Emergency Projects

Because it was a national organization and well organized—some would say over-organized—the CCC could always be called on to aid in disaster situations.

Firefighting

Wisconsin CCC boys were often called into action as firefighters. Sometimes fires burned near camps, while other times enrollees traveled a long way to put out a blaze. David S. Rouse recalled when his commanding officer asked for volunteers to fight a forest fire in northern Wisconsin close to the Brule River region several hundred miles north of Devil's Lake. Rouse, along with about twenty others, volunteered. When the recruits from Devil's Lake arrived at the host CCC camp north of Solon Springs, they learned that volunteers from other CCC camps were there as well. Rouse even met one of his Milwaukee friends assigned to Camp Riley Creek. The pair had a long visit comparing notes about CCC life. The next day, Rouse and his friend were assigned to firefighting details. Rouse's job was to wear a five-gallon watering can on his back and work with a mop-up crew to douse any smoldering embers. Rouse also helped cut a firebreak through the woods using axes, grub hoes, saws, and bulldozers. The plan was to completely encircle the forest fire zone. Rangers from the Brule River District directed everything. Rouse's group stayed in the area for ten days, helping where they could.[6]

Men on the hunt for *Ribes*, a genus of flowering plant that includes species of gooseberry and currants. *Ribes* host the white pine blister rust harmful to pine forests in North America. WHI IMAGE ID 42580

Flood Relief

During the winter of 1937, the Ohio River flooded, causing tremendous devastation in the surrounding watershed. The Sparta District immediately volunteered the resources of the district to aid with flood relief. The district offered 450 trucks and 900 officers, cooks, foremen, leaders, and truck drivers to help with the many problems the flood caused. CCC district leadership marshalled the men and resources into battalions, which they assembled at Camp McCoy. From there, men and supplies were sent to Illinois, Missouri, and Arkansas, states where the flood had caused the most damage. Though pressed into service quickly, the CCC men performed their duties admirably. According to one historian, "the battalions behaved in such an exemplary manner that the mission was accomplished with minimum confusion and damage of equipment."[7]

12

Forestry and Fish Hatchery Work

National Forest Work

At one time between 1933 and 1942, twenty-three CCC camps were active within the vast boundaries of the Nicolet National Forest in northern Wisconsin. Twenty-two of them were regular camps in which young, unmarried men were assigned to CCC service. The only outlier was Camp Phelps, where World War I veterans lived apart from regular enrollees but carried out similar assignments.

Recruits stationed in the Nicolet could expect to find themselves taking up many different jobs. In 1936, for example, the boys out of Camp Alvin near Alvin, Wisconsin, planted fourteen hundred acres of trees, built fifteen miles of truck trails, and laid five miles of roads. They also built fire towers and fought forest fires. And as if all that were not enough, they also stocked fifteen thousand fish in area lakes, planted deer browsing plots, and fed deer during the winter months.[1]

No matter what sort of jobs they did, however, the CCC men assigned for service in the Nicolet had their work cut out for them. Nor did the results of their efforts take immediate effect. When the forester Jay H. Price first cast his eyes on the Nicolet and Chequamegon forests in 1937, he described them as "sorry sights indeed. The evidence of old burns was everywhere and aspen was coming up. The plantings done by the CCC were still hidden by fireweed."[2] Conditions in the forests improved as a direct result of the CCC. The program is given credit for "establishing the Chequamegon-Nicolet Forest as a viable and productive area. . . . The CCC

Men at work in a northern Wisconsin forest. COURTESY OF STEVE SYLVESTER

boys performed many duties including fire control, tree planting, road construction and maintenance, telephone line installation, timber stand improvement and surveying. Much of the work done by the CCC is still evident today."[3]

On occasion, the CCC teamed up with the Works Projects Administration (WPA) to create park structures in Wisconsin. CCC recruits from Camp Nine Mile in Eagle River partnered with the Works Progress Administration to build the Franklin Lake Campground. There they constructed trails, roads, campsites, and buildings. Much remains of what was accomplished at Franklin Lake, as the campground has the largest grouping of rustic style buildings (log, stone, open porches, wide overhangs, exposed rafters) in Wisconsin's national forests.[4]

CCC companies in the Northwoods were on the constant lookout for fire. Watching for and controlling the spread of fire was part of everyday life for recruits stationed in areas where fires were a threat to themselves and the surrounding communities. One of the best ways to control forest fires was to build fire towers as a means for spotting a fire before it became

TREE PLANTING TECHNIQUE

Planting trees required hard labor, cooperation, efficiency, and a lot of time. Lawrence Kant recalled these details about tree planting:

> The tree planting detail was on the move by 6 a.m. Usually 180 men in the group. Each man had a grub hoe to carry over the three-mile hike, uphill and downhill, through swamp after swamp (there was two feet of water in those swamps) and finally dry land, (and wet feet). Then the men would line up, six feet apart, and move forward two paces on command and remove the sod from a four-foot square and then on command advance two more paces and dig another square. At the end of six hours, each man would average 55 holes; his hands would have a few new blisters, but the pain would ease on the long walk back to camp and that familiar Uncle Sam meal.
>
> After a night's rest, comes the dawn in the swamp. Gosh, how the arm muscles ached. But after chow, it was off to the woods on the double, with a box containing 50 six-inch trees and a long metal bar with a sharp flanged bottom. Then the men would fan out again, six feet apart and advance two paces (9 feet) and jab the metal bar into the previously grubbed hole, stick in a tree and firm it up with the heel of one's shoe. On an average day, one man could plant 500 trees (supporting crews would bring additional trees up in 250-pound boxes) a day and the ordeal continued day after day, rain or shine, until two or more inches of snow covered the ground . . . [and] those trees were not planted in open fields, but amidst standing trees.[5]

unmanageable. This brief entry in the *Oshkosh Daily Northwestern*, printed on September 13, 1933, described the construction of a fire tower at Camp Beaver: "An 80-foot fire tower is being constructed under the direction of the foresters. Camp Beaver, CCC, Company 1604."

ROAD BUILDING

Road building was no simple affair. In his journal, J. Allen Spoolman described how the CCC boys built a road.[6]

Monday, April 22, 9:45 p.m.

Two different jobs today. We went over on the Lenawee road this morning to widen it. After dinner we started brushing off the road Ahcey cleaned up last summer.

Tuesday, April 23, 9:30 p.m.

Landed a good job this morning with John Drudak setting out stakes for the road. In between times we piled brush.

Friday, April 25, 8:00 p.m.

By yesterday the cats, tractors, grader, and "boomers" . . . were tearing up, ripping, pounding and patting the ground into what began to look like a road. It's quite a process, this CCC road construction. First the surveyors and blazers, then the stake setters, then brushers. Then the mutter and clatter of the Cletrac, tearing and ripping stumps that are still wet with spring sap. Dynamiters blasting holes where once were partly decayed pine stumps or huge boulders, grumbling cats with their puny human stooges scurrying around throwing torn out stumps back in the woods. Then comes the gauge to level bumps and fill in potholes. A great rolling drum that works something like a hay rake. Then the Allis Chalmers dragging a reluctant lean wheel grader, which has a blade hanging from its belly that hardly hesitates at turning over a three-inch stump or a three-foot rock. They are the giants that make it possible for the "blue denim boys" to put out forest fires.

Friday, May 24, 11:00 p.m.

I got pulled from Tom's crew and put on Baggar's Thursday morning, cutting a road. We worked up to a tangent that had been left with no curve. So I had a chance to make a little practical use of what I learned about putting in curves from when we were at Brinks. But apparently they didn't trust me this morning as a ranger rode out with us—a "Rookie" just out of school from Syracuse. Anyhow, he didn't know what it was all about until I explained the procedure. I hate to think of what kind of curve he would have put in if I hadn't been there. Not conceited, just happy to think I knew something a tech foreman didn't know.

FIRE TOWER LOG EXCERPTS

Company 657 was stationed at Camp Elcho near Summit Lake in Langlade County. On June 20, 1933, the company erected a fire tower. The man in the tower kept a careful log. Here is a selection of entries from the log of the Basswood Hill Fire Tower built by CCC Company 657.

Friday, June 6, 1941

On Duty: 9:12 a.m.

Visibility 6–8 miles

Weather: Warm, haze

Wind: Moderate

Off Duty: 5:29 p.m.

Saturday, June 7, 1941

Off Duty

Sunday, June 8, 1941

Off Duty

Monday, June 9, 1941

On Duty: 7:57 a.m.

Visibility 15–18 miles

Weather: Cool, partly cloudy

Wind: Southwest, gentle-moderate

Off Duty: 5:30 p.m.

Tuesday, June 10, 1941

On Duty: 8:07 a.m.

Visibility: 15–18 miles

Weather: Clear, cool

Wind: Moderate-fresh

(Continued)

Off Duty: 5:30 p.m.

Wednesday, June 11, 1941

On Duty: 7:57 a.m.

Visibility: 8–10 miles

Weather: Cloudy, cool. Light rain. Moderate wind.

Off Duty: 6:00 p.m.

As these journal entries point out, the man in the fire tower experienced long stretches of boredom. Still, the watchman's eyes in the sky could spot a fire faster than any one on the ground, and a quickly spotted fire was one that could be more easily extinguished.

Camp Mondeaux River, Westboro

Camp Mondeaux River was established near Westboro between June 13 and June 20, 1933. It closed in 1937. Inspection reports conducted in 1933 (two of them) and in 1935 and 1936 revealed that the number of enrollees ranged from 207 (August 1933) to 151 (October 1936). The reports also revealed that no matter how many men were in camp, the recruits remained busy at their work. An inspection report from 1936 lists everything accomplished from June 30, 1933, to October 20, 1936:

- Telephone lines—10 miles built, 45 miles maintained
- Roadside cleanup—46 miles
- Timber stand improvement—2,000 acres
- Truck trails established—52 miles
- Truck trails maintained—85 miles
- Bridges built—5
- Tree planting—1,600 acres

- Tree plantation maintenance—2,000 acres

- Fire breaks created—18 miles

- Flowage cleanup—400 acres

- Fire suppression—700 man-days

- Logging—250,000 board feet

- Fish planting—60,000 fish

- Seed collection—58 bushels[7]

The CCC recruits at Mondeaux River kept at their work and in the winter of 1936–1937 began clearing the flowage basin for the Mondeaux River. They cut timber, cleared brush, and contoured soil. Beginning in 1937, WPA workers helped with the project. That May, the CCC and WPA began construction on a dam. In late 1937, the CCC and the WPA built a combination bath and clubhouse, plus a caretaker's home and a garage. By late 1938, the flowage was ready for flooding.

Oneida County Forest

On June 20, 1933, Company 654 arrived at Camp Blue Lake, four miles west of Rantz, Wisconsin, in the Oneida County Forest. What waited for Company 654 was a great deal of difficult labor, with a particular emphasis on planting trees and fire prevention. As one reporter noted at the time:

There are 220 men between the ages of 18 and 25 who will work in the Minocqua unit of the Oneida County Forest. They will be under Army control with Capt. William A. Murphy of Ft. Brady in command. The forestry superintendent is Stuart McCoy of Minocqua. The men live in squad tents of which there are 27, until their barracks are built. The majority of the men, 176 in number, are from Milwaukee, with the remainder from Northern Wisconsin. The bulk of the work will be for fire protection in getting the country in shape so that no fires will occur, or if they do, to make it possible to extinguish them immediately. When tree planting season starts in September, work in that line will be done.[8]

CCC and Fish Hatcheries

In collaboration with the WPA, the CCC improved and developed several of Wisconsin's fish hatcheries. The state of Wisconsin bought the Wild Rose Fish Hatchery in 1908 from a private fish farmer and began producing brook and brown trout in 1909. The hatchery, today a popular tourist attraction north of the village of Wild Rose, was built on a side hill with naturally flowing spring water, making it economical to operate. In the 1930s, the CCC shaped fieldstone and mortar walls for the rearing ponds in the hatchery. They also built a stone wall along Highway 22 that defines the entrance to the hatchery and remains intact to this day. Together, the CCC and the WPA erected the Thunder River Rearing Station, a state fish hatchery located in the township of Stephenson on Hatchery Road in Marinette County. Several vertical log buildings were constructed there between 1938 and 1940, including an office, garage, and four rearing stations.[9]

More fish hatchery work was done across Wisconsin by the CCC. The Art Oehmcke Fish Hatchery, formerly known as the Woodruff Hatchery,

Enrollees built this stone wall along the entrance to the Wild Rose Fish Hatchery near Wild Rose. COURTESY OF STEVE APPS

was located two miles east of Woodruff in Oneida County. The CCC and WPA worked on improvements at the hatchery between 1934 and 1939. The WPA crews handled the majority of the carpentry and masonry work, while CCC recruits from Company 654 developed new rearing ponds and landscaping.[10] Farther west, the Osceola Hatchery has operated as a state-owned fish hatchery since 1925. It adjoins the St. Croix River in western Polk County. CCC crews helped restore the hatchery in the early 1930s, including constructing seventy cement-walled raceways.[11]

13

SOIL AND WATER CONSERVATION WORK

The rolling hills of southwestern Wisconsin, known as the Driftless Area because the region was untouched by glaciers during the last ice age, include some of the richest and most productive agricultural land in Wisconsin. The quality of the soil attracted farmers accustomed to plowing up and down hills. When they did so over the Driftless Area, the environmental impact of their farming severely diminished the agricultural value of the land in less than a century. The authors of *Wisconsin Conservation History* wrote, "It took only 70 years, from the time of the first infusion of white settlers, to the early 1930s, for traditional farming methods to reduce the land around Coon Creek and elsewhere, from pristine to the brink of agricultural uselessness."[1] Traditional farming included plowing up and down steep hills rather than around them as contour cropping methods advised. These traditional farming practices resulted in the exposed soil being washed away when it rained.

By 1929 Congress had become aware of the widespread soil erosion problems facing the country. In response, it created ten federal-state agricultural research stations to study the causes of erosion and find solutions to prevent it. One was located in La Crosse, Wisconsin. In 1933, Congress appropriated five million dollars toward controlling soil erosion and created an agency in the Department of the Interior called the Soil Erosion Service (SES). When the SES was transferred to the Department of Agriculture in 1935, it became known as the Soil

THE CCC ON THE MULCAHY FARM

Carmen Mulcahy grew up on a farm near Fayette, Wisconsin, in Lafayette County. She remembered when CCC recruits from Camp Argyle worked on her father's farm in the late 1930s and early 1940s.

> I don't know if the CCC organization approached my father or he approached them to work on our farm. My parents were friendly with these young men. A CCC Camp was established near Argyle, where they resided. My parents were interested in nature and soil conservation. Some of these CCC boys did not have an agricultural background and they were interested in seeing the milking operation at our farm. They came to the house a number of times to get fresh milk. Sometimes they brought us leftover soup or bread in return.
>
> The work the CCC boys did on the farm included filling ditches and getting my folks started in strip cropping or contour cropping to stop soil erosion. My folks were among the first to do strip cropping. My father was very proud of an aerial photo of our farm showing the contour strips. The work of the CCC boys motivated some families to follow contour farming practices, which worked to protect the soil.[2]

Conservation Service (SCS). (The name was changed to the Natural Resources Conservation Service in 1994.)

Dr. Hugh Hammond Bennett, director of the SES, asked R. H. Davis, superintendent of the La Crosse research station, to pick a site for a soil conservation demonstration project. Davis selected the nearby Coon Creek watershed. Once he had his site, Davis enlisted the University of Wisconsin College of Agriculture to draft a report on erosion damage in the watershed and outline a plan for combatting soil losses due to water erosion. The lead architects of the plan included Noble Clark, associate director of research at the College of Agriculture; E. R. Jones, who chaired the Agricultural Engineering Department; Aldo Leopold, chair of the Department of Wildlife Management; and O. R. Zeasman, a University of Wisconsin soil conservationist.

These men knew the plan they eventually came up with would be a difficult sell to farmers in the watershed. It would be up to the scientists to prove that if Coon Creek farmers followed certain soil conservation measures, the farmers could not only restore their soil but enhance their yields as well. For his part, Dr. Bennett was so impressed with the plan that he designated it the pilot project, the number one soil erosion control project in America. The plan included practices to improve woodlands, pastures, and wildlife habitat, plus suggestions for better crop rotations, improved fertilization techniques, terracing, strip cropping, and streambank erosion control.

In addition to the social and scientific challenges erosion control presented researchers, there was an important policy challenge to consider. Initially, Roosevelt's vision for the CCC limited its work to public lands. But it soon became obvious that the majority of the soil erosion problems were occurring on private lands. To accomplish the intent of the law so that CCC enrollees could work on flood and soil erosion problems, Roosevelt offered an amendment that read: "The President may in his discretion extend the provisions of this Act to lands owned by counties and municipalities and lands in private ownership, but only for the purpose of doing thereon such kinds of cooperative work as are now provided for by Acts of Congress in preventing and controlling forest fires and the attacks of forest tree pests and diseases and such work as necessary in the public interest to control floods."[3] No specific mention of soil erosion or soil conservation was included in the amendment. To be in compliance with the language of the law, all CCC work related to soil erosion control came under the rubric of flood control structures, even though many of these structures, in reality, were for saving soil. Other widely adopted practices, beyond construction of small concrete dams, included contour strip cropping and terracing of steep hillsides to prevent soil erosion. Especially in the Driftless Area, much of the work had to be done on private lands to meet the criterion that "benefits must accrue primarily to the public interest (e.g., flood control) and not to private profit."[4]

Erosion control dams, like this one on the Skinrud farm in Springdale, were put in place by the CCC and helped sustain the agricultural usefulness of the land. WHS REFERENCE ID 142959

SOIL CONSERVATION CCC CAMPS

Several CCC camps in Wisconsin were established specifically to work on private land erosion projects. These camps were labeled with an SCS designation, which meant the enrollees were supervised by soil conservation specialists and other experts, including faculty from the University of Wisconsin College of Agriculture. The following is a list of CCC camps in Wisconsin with an SCS designation:

SES-1/SCS-1, Camp Coon Valley, Vernon Co.

SCS-2, Camp Gays Mills, Crawford Co.

SCS-3, Camp Ellsworth, Pierce Co.

SCS-4, Camp Argyle, Lafayette Co.

SCS-5, Camp Durand, Pepin Co.

(Continued)

SCS-6, Camp Viroqua, Vernon Co.

SCS-7, Camp Holmen, La Crosse Co.

SCS-8, Camp Independence, Trempealeau Co.

SCS-9, Camp LaValle, Sauk Co.

SCS-10, Camp Platteville, Grant Co.

SCS-11, Camp Mount Horeb, Dane Co.

SCS-12, Camp Richland Center, Richland Co.

SCS-13, Camp Irving, Jackson Co.

SCS-14, Camp Dodge, Trempealeau Co.

SCS-15, Camp Nelson, Buffalo Co.

SCS-16, Camp Bloomington, Grant Co.

SCS-17, Camp West Salem, La Crosse Co.

SCS-18, Camp Menomonie, Dunn Co.

SCS-19, Camp Cochrane, Buffalo Co.

SCS-20, Camp Ontario, Vernon Co.

SCS-21, Camp Highland, Iowa Co.

SCS-22, Camp Ettrick, Trempealeau Co.

SCS-23, Camp Hixton, Jackson Co.[5]

THE COON CREEK WATERSHED PROJECT

The Coon Creek watershed is twenty-two miles long and nine miles wide and comprises about ninety-two thousand acres. It covers three counties in southwestern Wisconsin (La Crosse, Monroe, Vernon) and has an outlet directly to the Mississippi River.

When soil conservation technicians sat down to devise a plan for controlling erosion in the Coon Creek watershed, they began by establishing a "general land use plan." The plan had many features. If a piece of pasture land had a 40 percent or greater slope (quite steep), cattle should be fenced out and the land planted to trees. If the property was wooded with a 25 percent or greater slope, the cattle should be fenced out and any gullies planted with cover crops. Cover crops included alfalfa, red clover, and various pasture grasses. For crop fields with 20 percent slope or greater, they should be seeded to pasture or hay. Ridgetop fields with 10 percent slope or less should be terraced with contour strips. All other fields with a slope of 3 percent or less should be contour strips, and flat fields were to use crop rotations.[6]

For farmers who signed up for the program, new fences, grass, alfalfa seed, and tree seedlings were provided free of charge. Bulldozers created terraces to redirect the flow of rain water. Farmers were taught how to plow *across* the slope rather than up and down. Four hundred eighteen farmers participated in the program, covering forty thousand acres of land. During the first year and a half of the project, approximately two hundred CCC boys did erosion control work at Coon Creek.[7]

It might be hard to believe, but the new soil conservation practices introduced to farmers along Coon Creek were radical to some people. This was especially true of the Norwegian farmers who had immigrated

An example of contour strip farming over a field in Vernon County. COURTESY OF STEVE PPS

to southwest Wisconsin in the middle 1800s, where they continued to farm as they had in Norway. Clarence Olson, a grandson of a Norwegian immigrant, grew up in hilly Vernon County. Olson remembered when the Norwegian farmers in his rural Westby neighborhood plowed their fields up and down the hills. Said Olson: "They were following the practice of generations of Norwegian farmers in Norway who followed a similar practice. . . . The rains in Norway were light rains, much more gentle than those these Norwegian immigrants faced when they moved to hilly southwestern Wisconsin."[8] The Norwegian farmers, by following the agricultural techniques of their ancestors, were causing their rich topsoil to wash down steep hills. Floods occasionally occurred in the valley as a result. The running water tore out fences, washed out roads, and destroyed farm buildings.

Still, even though farmers were not blind to what was happening, they were reluctant to sign up for a "government program." They were proud, hardworking people who were not about to have some government man tell them how they should plow their fields, what they should plant, and where they should pasture their cattle. When farmers agreed to do so, they were often kidded, or worse, ostracized, by their neighbors for working with government soil conservation specialists and the CCC boys who did much of the physical labor involved.[9] From three camps in Vernon County, the CCC built more than eighty structures in the surrounding area over a four-year period. One of them, the Guernsey-Bergin Dam, erected in 1936, was the largest dam structure built in Vernon County. (The dam was restored in 2011 after a 2008 flood damaged it.)[10]

Burt Bratberg was one of the CCC recruits assigned to various soil conservation projects in southwest Wisconsin. He served in the CCC from 1939 to 1940, living at Camp Holmen. Situated on ten acres of the M. F. McHugh farm just outside Holmen, Camp Holmen opened in August 1935. Bratberg remembered that his primary work was to introduce farmers to contour strip cropping, which meant plowing around the hills rather than up and down them. Bratberg served as a field assistant to agronomists from the University of Wisconsin who were helping farmers develop conservation plans. One of his duties was to gather soil samples from each strip of land, take them back to camp headquarters, and test them for pH (acidity), nitrogen, phosphorus, and potassium levels.[11]

Camp Mount Horeb, Mount Horeb

Company 1694 was dedicated to soil conservation work in southwestern Wisconsin. The company made its home at Camp Mount Horeb, opened on May 8, 1935, a mile north of Mount Horeb. One of the main responsibilities of the company was the construction of erosion control structures, including dams built from native limestone.

When he was eighteen years old, Louis Roedell came from the flat lands of Illinois to Camp Mount Horeb as a CCC enrollee. He was the rare recruit who found he enjoyed working in the kitchen more than in the field. Most enrollees hated KP, so they were only too happy to pass off their kitchen duties to Louis, who was equally eager to accept. Louis eventually worked his way up to baker—baking as many as twenty-one pies at a time in wood-burning kitchen ranges, along with doughnuts, cookies, and cakes. Louis was promoted to mess sergeant with added kitchen responsibilities. One of his main jobs was to prepare the food order and to make certain the mess hall was spotlessly clean. Another job for the mess sergeant was to make sure everyone was dressed properly for dinner—no work clothes were to be worn at meals.[12]

Camp Viroqua, Viroqua

Company 2610 was organized as a drought relief company in the summer of 1934. After a month of conditioning at Fort Sheridan, the company moved to Camp Illini (in Illinois), where the men lived in tents. In November of the following year, the company relocated to a camp seven miles west of Viroqua, where its mission changed to soil conservation work. When the CCC members arrived at Camp Viroqua, they made camp in a wheat field. Enrollees quickly set out to beautify their camp during their free time. Company recruits created flower gardens, a rock garden, and walkways made of native limestone.

In the summer of 1936, sixty men from the camp traveled to the Northwoods to fight forest fires. Most of the men in Company 2610 had never been in a forest, and few had experience with forest fires. In 1937, eighteen men from the company temporarily left camp to help solve problems caused where the Ohio and Mississippi Rivers had flooded.[13]

Beginning in 1940, James Skarda was a CCC recruit in Camp Viroqua. James's parents owned a small grocery store in Kendall, Wisconsin, and they were facing bankruptcy at the time. James's dad told him after James graduated from high school in 1940: "Jimmy, I can't help you go on to college, but I think you should join the CCC." Though James had never heard of the CCC, he took his father's advice. He started in the summer and early fall working in a limestone quarry near Viroqua. James was supervised by personnel from the SCS as he broke up limestone rock with sledgehammers. He and the rest of the company did so only after the rock was first dynamited into large chunks, which the CCC boys then pounded into softball-sized pieces before feeding the pieces into a stone crusher to make lime. Farmers spread the lime on fields to raise the pH for alfalfa crops.

James would do more than quarry work in the CCC, though. Good fortune came his way when, as James told it, "One day the office called me in and a person there said, 'I understand that you can type.'" James replied that he could. The person responded by saying, "The supply clerk is leaving, how would you like to take over?" It was excellent news for James. He remembered that "I got $45 per month as a supply clerk, which was $15 more than I previously received. Of course, I had to send $30 a month home, which my folks saved for me. And I got two stripes to wear on my sleeve, indicating that I was an Assistant Leader. It was an inside job, too. After a time as Supply Clerk, I was promoted to senior foreman. I now got $60 per month and was now a three striper. I was approaching eighteen years of age and I was a senior foreman."[14]

CAMP VIROQUA SONG

James Skarda recalled the following song that the boys at Camp Viroqua sang. He pointed out that this was the sanitized version, as the original had a few unprintable words.

CCC boys are we
Happy go lucky
Barefoot and free
We are the workers
We are not shirkers
We are the CCC boys are we.[15]

By 1940, World War II had begun in earnest across Europe. In America, CCC camps were closing as employment opportunities in the country improved. James saw it as time when he might leave camp and look for other work. He did not know at the time that he would be in the war very soon. He remembered that "after about a year, I left the CCC and moved to Chicago, where I found a job working in a clothing factory— Hart Schaffner Marx. I was in Chicago on December 7, 1941, when Pearl Harbor was bombed and after that I enlisted in the Navy, where I spent four years."[16]

BENEFITS TO SOIL CONSERVATION

Jimmy Bramblett, formerly Wisconsin State Conservationist for the National Resources Conservation Service, described the long-term benefits to soil conservation provided by the CCC: "I think what we learned through the CCC was that the Soil Erosion Service alone could not address the massive needs of soil erosion occurring across the country. We needed to have other individuals help us identify and prioritize natural resource management for soil and erosion control. Having the extra manpower was a great asset to help us demonstrate a unique private-public partnership—that of the federal government and the private landowner working together to carry out conservation practices."[17]

The 1930s were a time when partnerships of all kinds, between public and private enterprise and public and private citizens, were needed to accomplish important conservation goals in the United States. They were years of remarkable environmental devastation across the country. Residents of the Dust Bowl watched helplessly as millions of tons of soil, dried out with drought and churned up by agricultural practices, was blown into the wind where it blackened the sky. In the hill country of southwestern Wisconsin, water erosion raised havoc with farmers' fields, especially those farmers who insisted on plowing up and down the steep hills. With the help of the CCC, assisted by the newly formed SCS, working in cooperation with farmers and assisted by experts from the University of Wisconsin, things began to change for the better. It was the CCC and SCS who helped the nation see that soil and water were worthy of being protected and indeed *must* be protected if agriculture was to thrive.

14

State Park, County Park, and Municipal Projects

State Park Development

Before the CCC could move even a single shovelful of dirt in a state or national park, the National Park Service had to approve it. The NPS, the federal agency responsible for park development, divided the country into four districts. A district officer served as administrator for each district. Within each district, technically trained professionals, such as landscape architects and engineers, planned, monitored, and reported the activities for each CCC project. Additionally, inspectors worked closely with state park authorities to assure that CCC initiatives were in line with a given park's culture. Every detail of work activity was reported weekly or monthly to the district officers, who then routed reports to Washington, DC.

No new state parks opened in Wisconsin between 1933 and 1942. Several existing parks, however, were vastly improved by the CCC.[1] The first CCC camp to open in a Wisconsin state park did so in 1935. A great deal of preplanning and lengthy approval processes kept the CCC from starting work in state parks sooner. The NPS required that before a CCC camp could be established in a state park, the park needed a carefully developed master plan—something many parks previously did not have.[2]

State Parks

Seven CCC camps operated in state parks across Wisconsin. At Rib Mountain, Copper Falls, Perrot, Pattison, Peninsula, Wyalusing, and Devil's Lake State Parks, the CCC went to work building better facilities for guests and improving the land. With the help of landscape architects and engineers, CCC enrollees erected shelter buildings, concession stands, and sanitary facilities at state parks across Wisconsin. They cut trails and made stairways over steep terrain. Whenever possible, recruits used local stone and timber, learning a valuable craft along the way. As historian Cynthia M. Stiles noted, "As they worked side-by-side with expert craftsmen, the young men of the CCC learned the skills of stone cutting, masonry, carpentry and other trades—skills they would later take back into the workforce."[3]

Rib Mountain State Park, Wausau
Once known as Rib Hill, this four-mile-long ridge of quartzite rock near Wausau is claimed to be almost two billion years old. Until 1991, when a survey crew discovered that Timm's Hill in Price County is 1,952 feet above sea level, Rib Mountain, at 1,924 feet, was considered the tallest point in Wisconsin.[4]

This sign at the entrance to Camp Rib Mountain was designed by Howard James Hunn.
COURTESY OF JEANNE EVERT

In 1902, the Wausau Sandpaper Company was on the ground at Rib Mountain, crushing quartzite and making sandpaper and related products used for grinding and polishing. Twenty years later, the Wausau Kiwanis Club bought 120 acres of land on the top of Rib Mountain. Shortly thereafter, the Kiwanis Club bought 40 more acres. The Kiwanis Club then made inquiries to the Wisconsin Conservation Department as to the viability of creating a state park at Rib Mountain. They had good success, and in 1927, 860 acres of Rib Mountain was officially designated a state park. The park remained essentially undeveloped, though, until 1929, when a local Chamber of Commerce committee made plans to build a road to the top of the mountain. The road was completed in 1931.

On August 12, 1935, CCC Company 3649 established Camp Rib Mountain on the west bank of the Wisconsin River in the Town of Rib Mountain. From camp, the CCC created walking paths to further develop the existing road winding through the park. It built a campground, as well as a gazebo in a picnic area. Farther down the mountain, Company 3649 recruits had a hand in developing the Dells of the Eau Claire River County Park in Marathon County.

Interestingly, the CCC also did something at Rib Mountain that it did in very few other places across the United States. By 1935, Walter Roehl, a leader in the local Chamber of Commerce, had convinced the Wisconsin Conservation Department that Rib Mountain had potential as a ski hill. Soon the CCC was clearing ski slopes and installing a T-bar lift. Three years later, the first big ski event at Rib Mountain, the Central Ski Association Championship, was held on February 24 and 25, 1938. The event drew more than 465 participants and 3,000 onlookers. In December 1939, a new shelter house built by the CCC opened at the ski hill.[5]

The CCC left Rib Mountain in 1941. It left in its wake an accomplished legacy, as the CCC can largely be credited with not only helping develop Rib Mountain as a state park but also making it the popular ski destination it is today.

Copper Falls State Park, Mellen
In the early 1860s, Euro-American exploration for copper ore began on the site of what would become Copper Falls State Park near Mellen, Wisconsin. Native Americans had been mining copper in the region for

centuries, so prospectors believed they would find success in the area. The hunt for copper was no doubt fueled by the Union's need for the metal during the Civil War. Following the war, the tradition of copper mining in the area continued into the late nineteenth and early twentieth centuries when Wells M. Ruggles ran a mining crew on site. In 1902, Ruggles and his men dynamited their way through a forty-foot-high by one-hundred-foot-wide peninsula bedrock to redirect water from the Bad River, which often flooded the mineshaft. The blast area can be seen today from a footbridge near a picnic area. Ultimately, Ruggles and his crew found little copper ore, and the enterprise essentially failed.[6]

Kent Goeckerman, superintendent at Copper Falls State Park from 1973 to 2007, claims that the natural beauty of the area attracted visitors and drew volunteer laborers long before any CCC recruit or administrator had stepped foot on the ground. According to Goeckerman, "When the troops came back from World War I, they formed veteran groups and wanted to improve their local area through volunteer labor. They came out to what is now the park and put in the main park trails. They started advertising in the Midwest region for people to come up here, stay in the hotels, and go out and see Copper Falls."[7]

Before the land became Copper Falls State Park, it was owned by a power company that wanted to dam the Bad River to produce hydroelectricity.

This concession building at Copper Falls State Park was made by the CCC with lumber and stone harvested near the area. COURTESY OF SUSAN APPS-BODILLY

The dam was considered a threat by tourists and area veterans who were content to enjoy the landscape for recreational use. Goeckerman explained, "The veterans fought building a dam. They organized local people and lobbied the legislature to stop the dam. The legislature passed enabling legislation in 1928 so the old Wisconsin Conservation Commission could buy the park—between 500 and 600 acres. It became a state park in 1929. The World War I veterans kept it going into the early years of the Depression."[8]

CCC Company 692 arrived at Copper Falls State Park in November and December 1936. Recruits spent the following twenty-two months in the park, leaving in the fall of 1938. They were joined in camp by men from the Works Progress Administration (WPA). The CCC and WPA worked well together, with the older WPA members often mentoring the young men of the CCC. Goeckerman noted that "the WPA men would go home at night and come here during the day. A lot of these men had experience with masonry work, log building, and concrete work. They showed the CCC boys how to do this work."[9]

A stone fireplace at Copper Falls State Park built by the CCC. COURTESY OF SUSAN APPS-BODILLY

The CCC and WPA recruits at Copper Falls were not starting their work from scratch. They were picking up from where local veterans and volunteers had left off. Goeckerman described CCC and WPA efforts:

> They improved on the work that the World War I veterans had done. They tore out old bridges and put in CCC temporary bridges and then built permanent bridges across the Bad and Tyler Forks Rivers. Unfortunately, two of those bridges washed out when the river flooded in the 1940s. They built an observation tower. They constructed a large log shelter and concession stand, which is still standing. They built a bathhouse. They built two wing dams with gates that could divert the river's flow through an excavated half-acre pond to create a sandy beach. These wing dams could be periodically opened to direct the flow of the river to flush out the beach pond waters. The 1941 and 1946 floods ripped out the beach and damaged the bath house, which was later moved to Lucius Woods State Park at Solon Springs.[10]

As so often happened where CCC camps were pitched, the camp at Copper Falls had a positive impact on its neighboring community. As journalist Dennis McCann noted, "With their presence, and more important with the money they spent on food and supplies for their camp and their work over several years, they 'literally saved the town of Mellen from economic extinction during the post logging era and the Great Depression.'"[11]

Perrot State Park, Trempealeau

Located at the confluence of the Trempealeau and Mississippi Rivers in Trempealeau County, Perrot State Park has a rich cultural history. The park, which opened in 1918, is named after French explorer Nicholas Perrot, one of the first white people to explore the Upper Mississippi. A trapper and fur trader, Perrot helped develop trade relationships with Native Americans in the region. In the fall of 1685, Perrot and his men camped on the site of what is now the state park that bears his name. Later, in 1732, the French built a fort at the site of Perrot's campsite that was used until 1737.

Almost two hundred years later, in the summer of 1935, CCC Company 2606 opened Camp Perrot, where they remained until the summer of 1937. The first task assigned to the new company was to move trees from one area to another in a park that was scheduled to flood when a new lock and dam on the Mississippi River was completed. Additionally, the CCC cut hiking trails to the top of Brady's Bluff and Perrot Ridge; they built retaining walls and bridges, and constructed a shelter on top of Brady's Bluff using rock from a quarry near Trempealeau.[12]

Pattison State Park, Superior

Prior to 1935, Pattison State Park, opened in 1920 near Superior, had only a small picnic area, a few wooden overlooks, pit toilets, and a park ranger's cabin. Within the boundaries of the park is Interfalls Lake, which was once a very large lake. A dam constructed in 1928 made the lake bigger and created a muddy, weedy shoreline. On July 25, 1935, Company 3663 made camp at Camp Pattison in what is now known as the Little Manitou Falls picnic area. Over the next seven years, several thousand CCC men transformed the park. They put in sewer and water systems, planted trees, built three miles of foot trails, and removed old roadbeds. On top of that, they quarried rock, which they chiseled into blocks used to build a park shelter, nature center, and bathhouse. The CCC also drained Interfalls Lake, rerouted the Black River channel, and hauled sand from Lake Superior to create a beach.[13]

Peninsula State Park, Fish Creek

In 1909, the Wisconsin legislature, for less than twenty dollars an acre, purchased land in Fish Creek that would a year later be officially recognized as Peninsula State Park. During the 1920s and 1930s, the first game farm in Wisconsin operated in the park, where workers raised pheasants. In 1921, a nine-hole golf course was established at Peninsula, offering golfers dramatic views of Green Bay and the surrounding area.[14]

On August 10, 1935, CCC Company 3648 arrived at the newly established Camp Peninsular, built on property north and west of Gibraltar High School in Fish Creek. Upon arrival, the boys set up used army tents, creating a tent city. Construction soon began on more permanent camp buildings, including the following:

Four barracks (each 20 × 30 feet)

Garage (22 × 40 feet)

Two latrines (each 20 × 36 feet)

Pumping and light plant building (16 × 16 feet)

Recreation building (20 × 100 feet)

Mess hall and kitchen (20 × 120 feet with a 20 × 40 foot wing)

Officers' quarters (20 × 50 feet)

Foresters' quarters (20 × 90 feet)

Army office and orderly building (20 × 30 feet)

First aid and medical building (20 × 30 feet)

Bathhouse (20 × 36 feet)

Warehouse (20 × 40 feet)

Using local lumber and other building supplies, local carpenters and contractors in Door County constructed the buildings.[15]

The camp's educational director organized an array of course offerings to CCC recruits. Interested enrollees could take up everything from typing and shorthand to courses in agriculture, physics, chemistry, music, mathematics, algebra, high school English, spelling, first aid, and an assortment of crafts such as woodcarving and leathercraft. Courses and workshops were taught by local teachers.[16]

When they were not in class or at a workshop, the CCC recruits at Camp Peninsular were busy in the field. Before Camp Peninsular closed in 1937, enrollees built almost three miles of park roads, nearly fourteen miles of horse and hiking trails, and a stone and frame bathhouse (complete with four toilets) at Nicolet Bay. The CCC also developed three parking areas, improved eight acres of picnic grounds, created forty campsites for tents and trailers, improved the beach at Nicolet Bay, and constructed a ski jump. Two hundred acres of poison ivy was also cleared in an effort to eliminate gooseberry and black currant shrubs (to help control white pine blister rust). In addition, like other CCC recruits in Wisconsin's state parks and forests, the young men at Peninsular fought a forest fire or two. In 1936, the CCC built the Eagle Bluff panoramic viewing area, which afforded park visitors a stunning view of the peninsula and islands to the west of the park.[17]

The CCC camp in Peninsula State Park was a boon for Door County residents. Not only did locals teach classes and workshops in the camp, but unemployed stonemasons, carpenters, and others with trade skills worked with the CCC on several projects.[18]

Wyalusing State Park (Nelson Dewey State Park), Wyalusing

Located at the junction of the Mississippi and Wisconsin Rivers in southwestern Wisconsin, the land that is now Wyalusing State Park was once parkland owned by the Robert Glenn family. After a report commissioned by the Wisconsin legislature recommended the land be set aside as a state park, the legislature approved purchase of the land in 1912. What is now Wyalusing State Park was established in 1917, though it was known at the time as Nelson Dewey State Park. The name was changed to Wyalusing in 1937.

In July of 1935, CCC Company 2672 arrived at Camp Nelson Dewey and stayed there until 1937. Wooden structures were built for housing the CCC enrollees. Also constructed were an officers' quarters, a mess hall, a latrine, an infirmary, a recreation hall, and a supply depot. The CCC built park roads and trails and started construction of the Peterson Shelter, which was later completed by the WPA. The CCC made stone fireplaces in shelters and in the picnic area, as well as a kiosk, where information about CCC work is still on display. A bronze plaque commemorating the CCC and its achievements at Wyalusing is located near the outdoor group camp area.[19]

Devil's Lake State Park, Baraboo

Devil's Lake State Park, opened in 1911, is one of Wisconsin's oldest state parks—only Interstate State Park (1900) and Peninsula State Park (1910) are older. The park, near Baraboo, has a remarkable geological and cultural history, made all the more so by the fact that one of the famous Ringling Brothers owned a summer home on the lakeshore at one time. Several hotels were constructed on the lake in 1866, and a railroad to transport guests was completed in 1873. At the end of the nineteenth century, quarries operated near the park, one of which would later be useful to the CCC for building park projects.[20]

CCC Company 2669 arrived at Devil's Lake State Park in 1935. The company's nearly two hundred men came from locations in Wisconsin,

The CCC built this wood and stone structure at Devil's Lake State Park. COURTESY OF STEVE APPS

Illinois, and Michigan. A year earlier, some of them had been members of CCC Company 2615, located near Milwaukee, where they helped construct the Honey Creek Parkway and other projects.[21]

David S. Rouse was eighteen years old in 1935 and had just graduated from a Milwaukee high school. He had no job and little hope for finding one. Coming from a large family that was often on welfare, Rouse saw nothing but a bleak future as he, like many Americans, continued to endure the crushing effects of the Great Depression. David recognized an opportunity when he saw it, though. He signed up for a six-month hitch in the CCC and soon found himself at Camp Devil's Lake living in a six-man army surplus tent until barracks were constructed.

A rustic life in the CCC, even though it came with steady pay and regular meals, was not for everyone. Rouse recalled the difficulty some young men had in adjusting to camp life. Some could not tolerate being away from home. Rouse wrote, "Loneliness and homesickness hung over our wooded area like a light fog, blanketing the lowlands of our minds."[22]

Work at Camp Devil's Lake included planting trees, digging ditches, building a parking lot, establishing and improving hiking trails, and building a bathhouse. The bathhouse proved a major undertaking. The CCC boys' first step was tearing down the old structure. The new bathhouse was to be constructed of stone, so next the CCC enrollees were taught to remove stone from a nearby quarry and to shape the stones to show off their natural brilliance. Work at the quarry, difficult and backbreaking labor, began late in 1935. One advantage of working in winter was the ability to move rock from the quarry with sleds.[23]

County Parks

Just as the CCC made invaluable contributions to the development of state parks in Wisconsin its work with county park development was also laudable. Two county parks in Wisconsin benefited from CCC planning and labor: Dells of the Eau Claire River County Park and Goodman County Park.

Dells of the Eau Claire River County Park, Plover

Dells of the Eau Claire River County Park, in Marathon County, opened in 1923. Through its 190 acres of picturesque landscape winds the Eau Claire River. The Eau Claire Dells and its unusual rock formations, along with dramatic tumbling waterfalls, draw visitors to the park.

CCC Company 3649 started work in the Dells of the Eau Claire River County Park in 1935. Although the company devoted a majority of its time and resources to improvements at Rib Mountain State Park, it still did a great service to the county park. The CCC began construction on a 120-foot bridge in 1936, using stone quarried and handpicked locally and adding rails, posts, and decking. Another major CCC achievement in the park was the so-called Combination Building, a structure of logs and stone that included open and closed shelter spaces, a concession store room, a pumphouse, and toilets. The CCC also built the north park entrance and hiking trails, planted trees, and created a scenic overlook.[24]

Goodman County Park, Athelstane

Company 1696, stationed at Camp Dunbar in Marinette County, started on additions and improvements to Goodman County Park in 1936. The 240-acre park surrounds the Upper Peshtigo River at Strong Falls.

At Goodman County Park, the CCC built a log shelter with a fireplace at each end, plus a shelter house for small groups. Recruits also built a caretaker's cabin, garage, and workshop, all while landscaping the area.

MUNICIPAL PARKS AND PROJECTS

Though it might be hard to imagine, the CCC did important work in populated municipal areas during its years of service. While we might associate the CCC with deep forests, tree planting, fire towers, dams, and soil conservation, the CCC also built things such as swimming pools, which it did in Mineral Point and Viroqua.

Six CCC camps operated in Milwaukee County, employing about two hundred men each.[25] CCC recruits in the area did everything from build bridges to improve Lake Michigan's shoreline.[26]

Estabrook Park, Milwaukee

The CCC operated in Estabrook Park from 1934 to 1937. There the CCC cut paths, built stairwells, and put up fences. The CCC also cleared a fifteen-hundred-foot rock ledge on the Milwaukee River, which flows through Estabrook Park. Once the ledge had been prepared, the CCC built a flood control dam that included a rock spillway and flood control gates.[27]

Kletzsch Park, Glendale

In May 1935, a CCC camp was established at Kletzsch Park. The CCC stayed at the camp through the summer and fall before leaving in November. Recruits accomplished a great deal during their short stay. Not only did they build a shelter, they also built a new dam across the Milwaukee River. To do so, the CCC used reinforced concrete and followed a design that included a fish ladder built into the face of the dam. In addition to the benefit the ladder provided the fish, it also had the appearance of a natural waterfall.[28]

Sheridan Park, Cudahy

Located in Cudahy, Sheridan Park was once the estate of Patrick Cudahy, a Milwaukee industrialist whose family later donated the land to the city of

Cudahy for use as a park. Originally called Cudahy Park, it was renamed Sheridan Park in 1920 in honor of Civil War general Philip Sheridan.

Sheridan Park was the home of CCC Company 1644. The CCC boys assigned to it constructed park roads and trails. They also built concrete piers, or jetties, into Lake Michigan.[29]

Whitnall Park, Franklin

The CCC established Camp Whitnall in Whitnall Park in 1933. Like so many camps, Camp Whitnall was first a tent city. It didn't take long, though, for barracks, latrines, a mess hall, plus equipment and repair sheds to be constructed. The CCC built roads and bridges at Whitnall Park, where the men also dug lagoons, cleared streams, and built dams. Enrollees moved and rearranged tons of soil and planted thousands of trees and shrubs.[30]

15

THE UNIVERSITY OF WISCONSIN
ARBORETUM

John Nolen, a Madison landscape architect, proposed adding an arboretum to the University of Wisconsin in 1911, but his idea didn't become reality until several years later. In 1925, Michael Olbrich, a Madison attorney and nature enthusiast, and the Madison Parks and Pleasure Drive Association began raising money for the creation of parks in Madison. The goal was to preserve open space in the city and maintain access to its abundant lake shores. Olbrich's vision included support for an arboretum "that might also be a wildlife sanctuary, experimental forest preserve, protected area for sacred Native American sites, a place to experiment with re-establishing historical Wisconsin landscapes, and a refuge from the city."[1]

By 1927, Olbrich had convinced the University of Wisconsin Board of Regents to help finance the purchase of an arboretum. The first 246 acres of the arboretum, however, were not acquired until April 26, 1932. The land, which would become the Curtis Prairie, had been farmed and was regularly plowed with corn, oats, and pasture in rotation. Before Madison was selected as the state capital in 1836, the surrounding landscape had been dominated by oak openings and marsh, with the ground cover consisting of prairie grasses, prairie forbs (wild flowers), plus some shrubs and oak brush.[2] With additional purchases, the University of Wisconsin Arboretum acreage grew to its present size of 1,260 acres.

After years of planning, the Arboretum was dedicated on June 17, 1934. At the dedication event, Aldo Leopold, the Arboretum's research director,

The stone entrance to the UW Aboretum was constructed by enrollees living at Camp Madison. COURTESY OF STEVE APPS

outlined its purpose "of re-establishing 'original Wisconsin' landscape and plant communities, particularly those that pre-dated European settlement, such as tall grass prairie and oak savanna."[3]

WISCONSIN EMERGENCY RELIEF ADMINISTRATION

The Wisconsin Emergency Relief Administration (WERA), a state relief agency, almost immediately started an initiative to place workers at the Arboretum. Funded with federal money, the program was, like the CCC, designed to put out-of-work men into steady jobs. With the WERA and its workforce in the picture, the Arboretum became known as Camp Arboretum.[4] Officials with the WERA suggested a list of possible projects at Camp Arboretum that included the construction of a road through Arboretum property, pond excavation, and more. Potential WERA workers, most of whom were transients and stayed at a downtown Madison shelter, would shoulder the labor. In July of 1934, a group of laborers set up tents at the Arboretum, and by October of that year, ten wooden barracks had been constructed, with all costs covered by the WERA.

The plan was for Camp Arboretum to house up to 350 men for two years. But there were problems. The WERA had difficulty obtaining adequate funding from the federal government, especially for expensive projects such as road construction. And labor was not dependable, as many men in the WERA were drifters who left camp before a job was completed.[5]

CAMP MADISON, MADISON

To bring some stability and consistency to work at the Arboretum, its executive committee turned to the CCC. After the committee had familiarized itself with the CCC and its mission, it sent a letter to the University of Wisconsin Board of Regents asking the board to replace the transient workers at Camp Arboretum with a "Park and Forestry Service Civilian Conservation [Corps] Camp."[6]

The board granted the request. An advance party of CCC enrollees in Company 2760 got to Madison in the first days of August 1935. The main body of the company was right behind them, arriving by truck on August 16. Company 2760 had been at CCC Camp Honey Creek in West Allis. With everyone accounted for, 180 enrollees, plus about twenty army personnel, including cooks, supply personnel, and other administrative support staff, were stationed at the camp.[7]

Camp Madison, as the Arboretum camp came to be called, had a different character than other CCC camps in Wisconsin or the United States. For one thing, Camp Madison was the only CCC camp in America operating on university land. Company 2760 was also the only CCC company in the country charged with creating an arboretum. As historian Franklin E. Court noted, "Almost everything that distinguishes the Arboretum today can be traced back to those CCC years."[8]

One of the first things Company 2760 did at Camp Madison was refurbish and clean up the wooden barracks left by laborers and the WERA. The company ate in a mess hall housed on the first floor of a barn on Arboretum property. The rest of the barn was used by National Park Service personnel for their headquarters. The army set up its headquarters and a clinic in one of the barracks.

Camp officials provided enrollees with educational and leisure time activities. Aldo Leopold sometimes came by in the evening and provided instruction in archery. The camp also housed an extensive library. Sports, too, were of great interest to company recruits. Molly Fifield Murray, a former program and outreach manager at the Arboretum, recalled that the boys at Camp Madison "had a baseball team [and] a basketball team, and at one time or another they were champions in each. They played a lot of baseball."[9] Murray added that CCC recruits were exactly what the Arboretum needed in the 1930s, noting that "the Arboretum was happy to have the CCC rather than the transients because the CCC boys were committed for a minimum of six months so they could expect the guys to learn something and know what they were doing. With the transients, they might work a couple days and then be gone. So it was much better than what we had."[10] Between 1935 and 1941, Company 2670 built roads, constructed maintenance buildings, developed foot trails, dredged ponds, planted trees and shrubs, and raised stone shelters and stone walls. Their work was overseen by nationally known prairie ecologist Theodore Sperry, a specialist in the root systems of prairie plants. Sperry was employed by the National Park Service to help with prairie restoration work at the Arboretum. Leopold, who had read about Sperry's work in this highly specialized area, knew Sperry was the man the Arboretum needed to help develop its native plant communities.[11]

The innovative restoration program that founded sixty prairie acres, later known as the Curtis Prairie, at the University of Wisconsin Arboretum was not just original. It was groundbreaking, the first human-made prairie in the world. Norman Fassett, a professor of botany at the university, is credited with the idea of creating a prairie at the Arboretum.

Workers created experimental plots in an area of the Arboretum that had been a pasture. Getting native grasses and plants into the plots proved to be a challenge, involving an enormous amount of manual labor to collect and plant materials. It was just the sort of work suited to the CCC boys at Camp Madison. In their history of the Arboretum, Thomas J. Blewett and Grant Cottam wrote that "plant materials were collected in the fall of 1935. Hay and sod were collected in a low prairie near Mazomanie, on a dry hill slope and wet meadow between Sauk City and Mazomanie, on a dry hill slope 4½ miles west of Middleton, and on the sand plains northwest of Spring Green. To acquire western prairie species, Dr. Fassett assisted with the collection of shrubs and seeds on the bluffs of the Mississippi

River at Hager, and additional seeds were collected on the Mississippi River terraces near Lake Pepin and north of Portage."[12] CCC recruits collected individual plants and seeds to plant in the new prairie and to grow into seedlings for later planting. Their work was made all the more difficult by dry conditions during the summers of 1935, 1936, and 1937. Those seasons were so dry that the CCC had to haul water from Lake Wingra to water the sixty-acre prairie.

Between 1936 and 1940, Sperry created a map detailing the location of some forty-two plant species planted in the prairie.[13] His bold vision came to life in Madison in a way that had never been done before, made possible in no small part by the CCC. Sperry's creation also endured long after the CCC had left Madison. As Molly Fifield Murray explained it, "Sperry created a master plan. . . . He was doing the experiments [with prairie plots]. No one had ever done this before. Sperry came back here when he was eighty years old and could still find his plots. He proved that you could plant a prairie."[14]

In addition to creating the prairie, CCC enrollees planted several wooded areas, including the Leopold Pines, Wingra Woods, and the Galistel Woods.[15]

The Curtis Prairie at the UW Aboretum as it looks today. COURTESY OF STEVE APPS

Benefits of the CCC to the Arboretum

The enduring legacy of the University of Wisconsin Arboretum also re-
flects the legacy of the CCC in Wisconsin. The two are forever linked.
Molly Fifield Murray summed up CCC accomplishments at the Arboretum in this way: "They planted everything; they planted all the pine trees,
they planted all the maple trees. The CCC boys were committed to being
here. They were committed to working. The government brought in equipment—bulldozers, tractors, steam shovel-dredges. They brought things
with them that were really helpful to getting a lot of things done that the
university couldn't afford. There wouldn't be a University of Wisconsin
Arboretum without the CCC."[16]

PART IV

CRITICISM, SUCCESS, AND ENDING

16

THE CCC AND ITS CRITICS

Though the CCC is remembered today as one of the most successful and popular government programs in US history, it had its critics. Labor unions opposed the CCC for fear that it would fill good jobs with nonunion workers. The influential Socialist Party joined organized labor in opposition to the CCC on the grounds that the CCC would have little effect on the nation's unemployment numbers and that the camps "fit into the psychology of a Fascist state."[1] Politicians and their supporters who believed in limited government saw the CCC as yet another example of government overreach in action, another do-nothing federal agency soaking up limited tax dollars. In Wisconsin, C. L. Harrington, superintendent of Wisconsin's state parks and forests from 1923 to 1958, was among those who felt that it was unwise for state agencies to collaborate with the federal government. Said Harrington: "I don't like this taking money from Washington because then Washington can dictate to you what you can and what you can't do."[2]

Some educators also cast a skeptical eye toward the CCC. Some believed that the CCC placed too little emphasis on formal training or instruction in the classroom. Historian Paul W. Glad noted that "educators were concerned that the CCC administrators too often allowed character building to take the place of more formal training."[3] Indeed, US Commissioner of Education J. W. Studebaker urged CCC administrators to allow CCC recruits to attend vocational and other classes on Wednesday afternoons and on Saturdays. President Roosevelt did not approve of the idea.[4]

There were also those who drew unfavorable comparisons between the CCC and Nazi Germany. Some were nervous that the CCC too closely resembled Hitler's growing Youth Movement. Germany was one of the countries in Europe hit hardest by the Great Depression, with some six million people out of work.[5] As Hitler said in a 1933 radio speech, "The misery of our people is horrible. . . . To the hungry, unemployed millions of industrial workers is added the impoverishment of the whole middle class and the artisans."[6] The same could easily be said of the United States and its unemployed. Roosevelt set out to combat the problem of unemployment with the CCC, while Hitler organized unemployed young men into youth camps. The similarities were striking, though there were obvious differences in ideology and practice, as the youth camps in Germany were far more militarized than CCC camps in America. Still, as people in the United States learned more about Hitler's Youth Corps and its propaganda-driven, military-style regimentation, they worried that the CCC might take on a similar character. But as John Garraty wrote in his history of the Great Depression, "This concern proved to be unfounded; indeed, the army undertook the task [of overseeing the CCC] with great reluctance and performed it with admirable restraint. It is also difficult to imagine how so large a program could have been set up in so short a time in any other way."[7]

Critics also questioned what, if anything, the CCC could do to help the environment. When the CCC was still in its formative years, Aldo Leopold criticized some of the program's activities. Leopold saw the CCC as narrowly defined and doing more harm than good because it lacked what Leopold described as an integration of conservation practices. In an article published in May 1934, Leopold cited a case in which one crew was cutting a grade along a clay bank, which permanently roiled a nearby trout stream, while another crew worked on improving that same trout stream. Leopold concluded from this that "the plain lesson is that to be a practitioner of conservation on a piece of land takes more brains, and a wider range of sympathy, forethought, and experience, than to be a specialized forester, game manager, range manager, or erosion expert in a college or conservation bureau. Integration is easy on paper, but a lot more important and more difficult in the field than any of us foresaw."[8] Leopold advised conservation administrators that they should avoid CCC practices that

Leopold considered detrimental to conservation and land management. These practices included "excessive clearing and burning of underbrush, planting of jack pines, and cutting of fire lanes. . . . [And a failure] to appreciate the need for an approach to game management and reforestation that [takes] into account the carrying capacity of the environment and the optimum balance between wildlife and forest."[9]

Leopold eventually underwent a change of heart when it came to the CCC. His biographer, Curt Meine, explained that over time Leopold's attitude toward the CCC softened as he saw the results of its good work, especially in Wisconsin. According to Meine, Leopold's attitude "changed starting in 1934. Especially at Coon Valley, where the CCCs were key to that effort's success, and at the UW Arboretum. Coon Valley was a complete contrast to his Southwest experience: it was a model for integration and coordination. And the Arboretum saw the CCCs engaged in pioneering ecological restoration work."[10]

Finally, some critics accused the CCC of discriminating against women and African Americans. Eleanor Roosevelt was a proponent of women's rights and urged her husband to open CCC enrollment to women. FDR did not acquiesce.[11] The fight for CCC integration also took place in Wisconsin, where the La Follette brothers, Philip and Robert Jr., opposed CCC racial discrimination and lobbied to establish a desegregated CCC camp. Though CCC legislation specifically stated that "no discrimination shall be made on account of race, color, or creed," camps were segregated, especially in the South. When the La Follette brothers asked Robert Fechner to consider the possibility of a desegregated camp in Wisconsin, Fechner turned them down.[12]

In general, however, public criticism of the CCC began to wane as program's popularity soared. In fact, the CCC, in the words of one historian, "quickly became too popular for criticism."[13] Those in Washington, Republicans and Democrats alike, had good cause to support the CCC when they witnessed the following things happening:

1. Governmental agencies worked together. The CCC involved the War Department, the Department of Agriculture, the Department of the Interior, the Department of Labor, and the Veterans Administration. Major governmental agencies

were more often than not in competition with each other for money and influence, so everybody gained during a rare moment of interagency cooperation.

2. The program was enacted quickly. The first CCC recruits were in camps only weeks after the passage of CCC legislation in 1933.

3. The CCC assisted families as well as enrollees. Of the $30.00 that a CCC recruit received each month, $25.00 was sent home to his family. Because many families were struggling to survive at the time, $25.00 fed people who might have otherwise gone hungry.

4. The CCC employed skilled local labor. Local experienced men were often hired to do work in CCC camps that required advanced skills. These workers lived near the camp in which they were employed, spending their workdays with the CCC and their evenings at home with their families.

5. The CCC had a positive economic impact on communities near its camps. The CCC bought food and supplies from local retailers, and enrollees spent their money in small towns across the United States.

Given the ringing endorsement the CCC received from the voting public, its mission to improve the environment, and the good it accomplished across America, it became difficult for even the most hardened government dissenter to voice public criticism of the program.

17

ACCOMPLISHMENTS AND ACCOLADES

CCC director Robert Fechner eloquently summed up the purpose and mission of his agency when he wrote in 1938 that "the keynote of the CCC program is service. It serves youth by giving idle young men jobs, an opportunity for work experience, practical training that fits them for private employment and improved health. It aids the Nation not only by building manhood, but by utilizing unemployed youth upon worthwhile conservation projects in forest, fields, and farms, which conserve and add to the national wealth."[1]

Two accomplishments that Fechner mention certainly stand out: enhancing the personal lives of several million young men and improving the natural environment, broadly defined. But other CCC accomplishments deserve recognition as well. The CCC pushed Americans to understand that long-term plans were needed to care for and protect the natural beauty and resources of the United States. And the CCC, and the New Deal in general, changed how people thought about the federal government and the role it played in their lives.

ENHANCING PERSONAL LIVES

The CCC had a positive and far-reaching impact on millions of Americans, many thousands of them in Wisconsin. Jerry Bayer, who served in the CCC at Camp Long Lake near Long Lake, Wisconsin, was grateful for the opportunities the CCC offered him and carried his experiences with him for the rest of his life. Bayer said, "My time in the CCC helped me in later life. I went through the cooking school at Sparta. It was all hands-on training. I wound up being the cook for the officers mess at headquarters. When I was discharged, I used my training to get a job at the Schroeder Hotel in Milwaukee as an apprentice cook."[2] David S. Rouse summed up the value of the CCC experience with these words: "I joined up as a boy and came out feeling like a man, with a sense of self-respect, dignity, and assurance that there would be a future for everyone in America."[3] When asked what he took from his hitch in the CCC, James Skarda replied, "I learned how to work and I developed some wonderful friendships. A fellow from Chicago who played baseball with me in Viroqua became a great friend. He was best man at my wedding."[4]

Joan Palmer, whose father, Maxwell, joined the CCC in 1938, provided a moving account of how the CCC transformed the life of one Wisconsin man and his family for the better. Joan wrote the following about her dad:

> My father, Maxwell Palmer, joined the CCC in 1938. At the start of the Depression, my grandfather was a custom cabinet maker in Madison. Obviously, the need for his skills dried up. The family dredged up $200 to pay the back taxes on the family homestead in Highland, WI, and moved there to ride out the Depression. In 1934, a CCC camp was opened just north of Highland.
>
> In the fall of 1938 when my father was a senior in high school, he joined the camp as soon as he turned 18. He lived at the camp, went to high school during the day, was camp secretary and taught English, typing, and math in the evenings and on the weekends. He never planted a tree. His wages supported his family.
>
> When Max graduated from high school in 1939, he transferred to the CCC camp in Platteville as their night medic—with no medical experience at all. He attended the Platteville Mining School during the day. His college experience ended when he ran out the two years maximum that you could be in the CCC program.
>
> In the 1940 census, Max's income for 1939 was listed as $371 and his father's at only $300. I am certain that the majority of Max's income went to support his family. Living at the camp also took financial stress off the family, with one less mouth to feed.

In May 1940 (at the end of the school term), Max enlisted in the army. He wanted to fly but at that time the military required two years of college and he had only one. After Pearl Harbor, he was allowed to test out of his second year of college and changed to officer status. He became a B-26 pilot and flew sixty-one combat missions over Italy and France.

The year of college as a CCC member put him a year ahead of his colleagues returning to school on the GI Bill. Max finished at the University of Wisconsin in mechanical engineering in less than three years and hit the job market ahead of the competition. He eventually became the head design engineer for the Fermi Lab in Illinois designing nuclear accelerators.

My father's older sister married a CCC boy from Alton, IL, who was stationed at the Highland CCC Camp.[5]

LETTER FROM CCC ENROLLEE UPON RETURNING HOME

Cecil A. Moeller of Pittsville, Wisconsin, wrote this letter to his sister and brother-in-law in Missouri shortly after he was discharged from the CCC on April 1, 1938. Among other places, Moeller served with CCC Company 2617 in Camp Sawyer near Winter, Wisconsin.

I've been pretty busy since I've come home with the fishing, brushing, planting, hoeing, and fencing. It's raining now so I haven't any excuse for not writing . . . we got our '29 Ford in pretty good shape now but it's not been run much since I've been home. We haven't got a '38 license on it yet. We are depending on the beans and pickles for a profit this summer. . . . I was in camp 20 months in four camps altogether. I've got a good honorable discharge . . . I have had several pretty fair jobs offered me since I was home but passed them up to help Dad this summer so he can get some building done this fall. Dad complimented me on my strength since I've been home. I chin myself with one arm, and raise a sack of flour with either arm. I was nearly the lightest fellow in

(Continued)

camp until we got rookies from Chicago. I weighed about 116 pounds stripped at about five-foot three height. I think of you by writing this letter, which is labor for me. So long. Cecil A. Moeller.

When the United States entered World War II in 1941, Moeller was drafted and served with the 101st Airborne. He was discharged in 1945. Though he survived the war, tragedy struck Moeller a few months after returning home when his car became stuck in a snow-covered ditch. While running the engine to keep warm, he died of carbon monoxide poisoning.[6]

Appreciating Natural Resources

Kent Goeckerman believes that the CCC had a profound and lasting impact on the way Americans treat the environment and use their natural resources. As Goeckerman put it, "The CCC had a tremendous influence on the environmental movement, which included changing people's attitudes toward the need for protecting and improving the environment."[7] Goeckerman's statement, informed by decades of professional experience, echoes an idea sometimes put forward by historians. Colin Taylor Higgins, who has studied the outcomes of various New Deal Programs in Wisconsin, wrote that "environmental changes certainly occurred in Wisconsin during the Great Depression, especially as a result of CCC-style conservation. These significant changes were also drivers of larger shifts in people's concepts of nature."[8] Higgins concluded that the CCC can in large measure be credited with creating the postwar environmental movement. The predominant view held by many Depression-era Wisconsinites was to cling to the old pioneer belief that people needed to civilize a "savage nature." The CCC program helped change this attitude to one of codependence between people and the environment.[9]

This is not to say that President Roosevelt and his administration were the passive beneficiaries of the CCC's hard work. On the contrary, Roosevelt and his CCC officials, keenly aware of New Deal skepticism, launched an extensive public relations program to promote the virtues of the CCC.

As Neil A. Maher noted, "The Corp's publicity department sent out thousands of press releases to newspapers across the country, hundreds of feature articles to nationally syndicated magazines, and dozens of pamphlets on CCC work projects to forestry, farm, and conservation organizations as well as to community groups, such as chambers of commerce and town councils."[10] In addition, the CCC created its own film production company in 1935 that released more than thirty films showing the work of the corps in the nation's forests, parks, and on its farms.[11] Not only did the CCC public relations machine keep the good works of the CCC on the minds of the American public, it also promoted the progressive idea of conservation. Maher explained that "as the Corps promoted its conservation projects during the early New Deal years, and as the national media publicized such work, ordinary Americans began to learn about natural resource conservation, many for the first time."[12]

By 1938, Fechner had come to recognize the effect the CCC was having on the topic of conservation across America. He wrote:

> As an organization for conserving the Nation's natural resources,
> the CCC has shaken the country out of the complacent lethargy
> with which it normally has viewed vitally important conservation
> problems. It has launched the Nation upon a conservation program,
> which if carried on in an orderly manner, eventually will take our
> forest and soil budgets out of the red. . . . In my opinion, the results
> achieved through the use of CCC men in advancing conservation
> projects have been—or soon will be—so great a dollar value as to
> offset the dollar cost of the program. . . . By giving thwarted youth
> opportunity to develop into healthy manhood under wholesome
> conditions which make for good citizenship, the Corps has strength-
> ened Democratic government. Its record demonstrates that the CCC
> is a sound national institution for conserving youth and natural
> resources.[13]

Not only did people learn about and come to appreciate the need for natural resource conservation as the result of CCC efforts, many individuals and organizations began planting trees on their own.

ACCOMPLISHMENTS OF
CAMP SHEEP RANCH, PHILLIPS

Camp Sheep Ranch, located near Phillips in northern Wisconsin, hosted 882 CCC recruits from 1933 to 1936. A writer for the Town of Emery Centennial Book said this about the accomplishments achieved there:

> The effort of 882 young men over a period of three years cannot help but make a lasting impression on the progress of the Conservation Movement. They chopped, they sawed, they dug, they scalped the sod, they planted, or in short, they worked to put idle acres to work.

Not surprisingly several women's groups took up the cause of the CCC. Many women leaders had spearheaded environmental improvement initiatives before the CCC came into existence in 1933. In 1905, for example, Lydia Phillips chaired the forestry committee of the General Federation of Women's Clubs. The forestry committee did tree planting and forest preservation work under the umbrella of an organization with eight hundred thousand members scattered across the United States. Margaret March-Mount, another leader in forest conservation work, led efforts from her Milwaukee office where she directed "conservational educational activities" for women's clubs. March-Mount promoted tree planting to garden groups, school-children, and other civic clubs. When the CCC brought greater visibility to the importance of conservation and tree planting, women's clubs' and other civic groups' efforts to encourage tree planting increased proportionally.[14]

Not only did tree planting and forest improvement gain traction among the general public during the Depression, but soil conservation did as well. Of course, the dust storm years of 1932 to 1939 were on the minds of many. It was apparent from the dark clouds of dust across the sky that agriculture had gone too far in its lack of concern for the nation's soil. The CCC planted windbreaks to prevent soil erosion and, with assistance from the Soil Conservation Service, introduced contour strip cropping to farmers. The CCC also built erosion control dams to combat water erosion on rolling hills.

They thinned the dense stands of young saplings that the remaining trees might become mature in a shorter time. They removed the culls and defective trees from the remnants of former stands to aid nature in bringing up a new forest. They started new forests on the barren hills, hills made barren not by axe or saw, but by the red enemy of the forest fire . . . They constructed fire lanes that will check the red enemy. They conserved the rushing waters where the trout play. . . . We must not forget that there has been a major social contribution made to the community, state and nation, for when youth joins hands in a common cause . . . ambitions are fostered, ideals formed and friendships cemented that the years cannot erase.[15]

A Changing Attitude toward the Role of Government

During the Depression, many rural people in Wisconsin were suspicious of the federal government and its involvement in their lives. There was also in rural communities a general distrust of state government.

The success of the CCC turned many heads and softened many of those attitudes. Having seen up close the results of CCC labor, rural Wisconsinites began to think differently about the role of the federal government and what it could accomplish. The prevailing rural attitude had been that anything connected to government was a boondoggle that wasted money, involved too much reporting and paperwork, and ultimately failed or at least did minimal good. The entrenched belief was that the free market and competition, without government intervention, accomplished more with less money.

The CCC was different. The corps overwhelmingly proved that it was possible for a federal government program to accomplish its ends in ways that had positive and lasting impacts in rural areas across the United States. When put to good use, taxpayer money could and did make a tremendous difference in the lives of people and the environment.

18

THE PROGRAM ENDS

I t was never the goal or the purpose of the CCC to keep its camps running indefinitely. The nature of its New Deal relief mission meant that in better times the CCC would look less attractive to job seekers and taxpayers alike. By 1939, when the CCC entered the last years of its existence, war clouds had begun to form over Europe and the Pacific. Job opportunities had begun to increase in the United States, and applications for the CCC were in decline. At the same time, Congress authorized the formation of the Federal Security Agency, which mandated the consolidation of several offices under the leadership of one director. As a result, the CCC lost its independent status. When Congress added $50 million to the CCC's appropriation for 1940–1941, taxpayers questioned the need for the organization in an improving job market. Indeed, when there was good work to be had in the private sector, it became clear that the CCC was in serious trouble. By late summer 1941, CCC enrollment had dropped from about three hundred thousand to around half that number.[1]

The CCC suffered an additional operational and personal setback when Robert Fechner died on January 1, 1940. James D. McEntee, who had been assistant director since 1933, became the director. McEntee did not defend the CCC from its critics in the same forceful and effective way that Fechner had done so successfully during his tenure. And in 1940, the CCC was in need of defending. Hitler had moved his army across much of western Europe and was threatening to invade Great Britain. Military spending in the United States shot up while unemployment numbers dropped significantly. Hundreds of CCC camps closed. When the Japanese attacked Pearl

Harbor on December 7, 1941, national defense became the top priority in Washington, DC. The same kinds of young men who had once volunteered for service in Roosevelt's Tree Army were now signing up to serve their country as soldiers in the next great war.[2]

A joint committee of Congress recommended that the CCC be abolished on July 1, 1942. Technically, it was not abolished, but defunded. Some $8 million was allocated to cover the costs of the liquidation of the CCC, with its properties going primarily to the War Department. On July 1, 1942, Fred Morell, the assistant chief of the US Forest Service, sent telegrams to all regional foresters in the United States. The telegram stated that Congress had passed legislation liquidating the CCC and that "the War Department would take over all the camps and CCC property and that all remaining CCC employees be furloughed or terminated . . . as soon as their services were not required to supervise enrollees, guard vacated camps and to handle property and reports."[3]

NATIONAL FORESTS AND CCC CAMP CLOSURES

When World War II began in 1941, the United States had more employment opportunities than people to fill them. Whereas the national forests, such as Chequamegon and Nicolet, had flourished with CCC help, with less money and fewer men due to the war, the CCC safeguarded the forests from fire and timber theft and did little else. As one newspaper put it, "The war years were described as a period of relative inactivity, necessitated by pared-down staffs of the ranger districts. The role was a 'custodial' one."[4]

ADDITIONAL CCC INFLUENCES

No program as large or as far-reaching as the CCC has since been organized in the United States. Federal programs have replicated its success, however, often by following the CCC model. In some ways, the CCC paved the way for such programs as VISTA (Volunteers in Service to America), the Peace Corps, and the Job Corps. In 1983, the Wisconsin legislature passed legislation creating the Wisconsin Conservation Corps, a much smaller organization. WCC members, both men and women, did not live in camps but lived at home as they carried out various conservation work projects around the state.[5]

The CCC continues to be remembered by many as a popular, useful, practical, and well-run federal relief agency. More than seventy-five years after the program was shuttered, the CCC's contributions to America are still visible over the land. Many of the physical structures that CCC recruits built in state parks still stand. So too is CCC labor evident in the contour strip cropping on hilly farm land and in the national forests that CCC members replanted one tree at a time. The CCC also deserves credit for some things that can't be seen. The program changed the hearts and minds of thousands if not millions of Americans when it came to prioritizing environmental preservation and conservation in the United States. Roosevelt's Tree Army also made it clear that the federal government could carry out a mandate efficiently and effectively. And, finally, it must never be forgotten that the CCC saved the lives of millions of young men and their families during a time when hope for better days had been all but blown, like so much soil, into the wind.

19

MEMORIES REMAIN

Today only a handful of CCC boys are still alive. Some are part of a robust effort being made to keep Depression-era memories alive, to help people remember the great contributions the CCC made to the United States during one of the country's greatest times of need. Testaments and monuments to CCC achievements are found in state parks, museums, and exhibits scattered across America. Several are in Wisconsin.

CCC STATUES

CCC commemorative statues can be found across the country. As of 2017, seventy-one exist. Pennsylvania has the largest number with seven. A listing of all the CCC statues in the United States can be found by visiting the Civilian Conservation Corps Legacy webpage.[1]

There are four such statues in Wisconsin: at Galloway House in Fond du Lac, at Devil's Lake State Park near Baraboo, at the Trees for Tomorrow campus in Eagle River, and at Fox River Park in Burlington. The most recent statue, erected at Fox River Park, was dedicated on September 30, 2015, and was made possible by a generous gift from the John & Ruth L. Kloss Charitable Trust.

The statue at Devil's Lake State Park was made possible by the determined efforts of Howard "Howdy" Thompson. Before passing away in 2011, Thompson, who had been a CCC enrollee, lobbied long and hard to raise funds for the statue. His dream became a reality on July 30, 2004, when the CCC statue at Devil's Lake was raised in dedication to the CCC and the young men whose hard work made it all possible. Credit for the statue at

CCC commemorative statues, like the one at Devil's Lake State Park, are located through-out the United States. To date, there are four such statues in Wisconsin. COURTESY OF STEVE APPS

Trees for Tomorrow belongs to Richard Chrisinger, a CCC veteran and major contributor who proposed the idea for a statue in 2013.[2]

CCC Museums

Museums and permanent exhibits commemorating the work of the CCC are located in twenty-eight states. Wisconsin has two CCC museums, one in Rhinelander in the Pioneer Park Historical Complex and one in Fond du Lac at Galloway House.

CCC Museum at Pioneer Park Historical Complex, Rhinelander

The CCC museum in Rhinelander's Pioneer Park Historical Complex opened in June of 1983 and was dedicated on September 21, 1983. It was a project of Wisconsin Chapter 23 of the National Association of CCC Alumni.

In 1981, Ken Elliott, who was president of Chapter 23, suggested the group raise funds to construct a building to memorialize the CCC's involvement in Wisconsin. The group solicited money from timber firms, wood processing companies, the US Forest Service, and CCC alumni. Trainees at the Blackwell Job Corps Conservation Camp did the carpentry work to frame a replica of a 1933 CCC barracks. The interior was finished by Chapter 23 alumni.

The museum offers a glimpse of CCC work with a vast collection of photographs contributed by former CCC members and their families. Visitors can also see a replica of typical sleeping quarters for CCC members, with the army cot, footlocker, and olive drab wool blankets. Additionally, a mess hall replica shows what it was like to eat in a CCC mess hall with two hundred other diners.

Cheryl Westbrook, a tour guide at the museum, said,

> Visitors to the CCC museum are amazed at the collection, especially the [number] of photos that have been donated. The donations keep coming in as well. A couple weeks ago we received a CCC footlocker, and someone donated CCC discharge papers for a former CCC member in their family. We have many schoolchildren visiting our

Mannequins on display at the Pioneer Park Historical Complex in Rhinelander model CCC and other government uniforms. COURTESY OF STEVE APPS. PHOTO USED WITH PERMISSION FROM THE PIONEER PARK HISTORICAL COMPLEX

museum. Among other things, I tell the kids that the CCC boys received but $5.00 a month, after most of their salary was sent home to their families. I ask the kids if they got $5.00 a month, would they be happy? They stare at me.[3]

Aprelle Rowski, a museum coordinator, added that "we have the logging museum that shows how the loggers came in and cut all the timber in the north, and we have the CCC museum that shows how the CCC boys came in and planted back the trees."[4]

The museum is open from the last week in May through the first week in September.

CCC Barracks at Galloway House, Fond du Lac

Located in the Historic Galloway and Village museum complex, this museum is open from Memorial Day weekend through Labor Day, plus weekends in September. Open for exploration is a replica of a CCC barracks similar to the kind a CCC recruit would have lived in. A life-size bronze CCC worker statue is also part of the exhibit.

CCC Alumni

CCC alumni groups emerged following the disbanding of the CCC in 1942. Many are in operation to this day. A prominent national group, Civilian Conservation Corps Legacy, previously known as the National Association of Civilian Conservation Corps Alumni, has its headquarters in Edinburg, Virginia, and publishes the *CCC Legacy Journal* six times a year. The journal's readers include CCC alumni, sons, daughters, and other relatives of CCC members. Researchers and historians interested in CCC activities also subscribe to the journal, which was first published in 1978. Since 2013, a digital version of the journal is available online.[5]

Local CCC alumni chapters are scattered across the country. Waupaca Area Chapter 54 received a charter from the National Association of Civilian Conservation Corps Alumni on December 1, 1981. At its fifth annual Christmas banquet, held December 3, 1985, at Oakwood Inn in Waupaca, Harland Hansen of the Pine River area in Waushara County read the memorable "Who Are We" essay written by an anonymous CCC alumnus:

Who Are We?

We are the young men of the 1930s who made up the Civilian Conservation Corps—1933–1942.

We are the men who mended the scarred land, the eroded fields, the muddied waters of our creeks and rivers and the depleted woodlands of our country.

We replanted our forests from Maine to California; we built fire trails to protect the old and new forests, cleaned out the diseased deadwood to protect the healthy and new trees; we fought forest fires and floods.

We built lodges in our national parks and campsites for our people to enjoy our beautiful country. We also built roads and trails in the parks, many of them in existence today.

We worked the quarries to produce the building stone needed to build the dams in our state and national parks; the same dams that stand today creating the lakes that have given recreation to campers, fisherman and family groups over the last 50 years.

We worked the quarries getting the rock to crush for limestone to be spread on the farmlands to sweeten the overworked soil to help restore productivity. From other quarries came the building stone needed for masonry dams and flumes, which controlled the rapidly eroding soil.

We were educated and given job opportunities, honor, respect and purpose in life.

All over the country the work we did with our hands, our minds and our bodies still stand today, as a monument to the youth of the 1930s and what we accomplished; bearing in mind that ninety percent of what we did was done by hand, pick, hoe, shovel, mauls, drills and wheelbarrows.

We put our mark on this land and that mark will still be seen for many more years to come.

As a generation we have much to be proud of, we have earned a place in history and speaking as an individual, I am grateful for having had the chance to be there.[6]

Notes

Chapter 1: Introduction

1. John A. Salmond, *The Civilian Conservation Corps, 1933–1942: A New Deal Case Study* (Durham, NC: Duke University Press, 1967), chap. 1, http://www.nps.gov/parkhistory/online_books/ccc/salmond/chap1.htm.

Chapter 2: The Great Depression and Natural Resources Abuse

1. Robert S. McElvaine, *The Great Depression: America, 1929–1941* (New York, NY: Three Rivers Press, 1993), 17–20.
2. Jennifer Rosenberg, "Flappers in the Roaring Twenties," ThoughtCo., https://www.thoughtco.com/flappers-in-the-roaring-twenties-1779240.
3. "Brief Timeline of American Literature and Events: 1920–1929," http://public.wsu.edu/~campbelld/amlit/1920.htm.
4. Errol Lincoln Uys, "Civilian Conservation Corps: Saving a Lost Generation of Young Americans," http://erroluys.com/greatdepression.html.
5. Ibid.
6. History.com Staff, "Dust Bowl," History.com, https://www.history.com/topics/dust-bowl.
7. E. L. Kirkpatrick and Agnes M. Boynton, *Wisconsin's Human and Physical Resources: A Graphic Presentation of Conditions Affecting Rural Rehabilitation* (Madison, WI: Research Section, Resettlement Administration, Region II, 1936), 35–6.
8. Irving Bernstein, "Americans in Depression and War," in *The U.S. Department of Labor Bicentennial History of the American Worker*, ed. Richard B. Morris (Washington, DC: US Government Printing Office, 1976), chap. 5, https://www.dol.gov/oasam/programs/history/chapter5.htm.
9. Wisconsin Historical Society, "Depression and Unemployment," *Turning Points in Wisconsin History*, https://www.wisconsinhistory.org/turningpoints/tp-045/?action=more_essay.
10. Wisconsin Department of Natural Resources, "Cultural History of Wisconsin's Forests," in *Statewide Forest Assessment 2010*

(rev. September 28, 2015), appendix B, https://dnr.wi.gov/topic/ForestPlanning/documents/AppendixB_100721.pdf.

11. James J. Colby, "New Conservation Era Dawns for Wisconsin: Drought Proves Spur," *Milwaukee Journal Sentinel*, November 25, 1937.

12. Wisconsin DNR, "Cultural History of Wisconsin's Forests."

13. Colby, "New Conservation Era."

14. Ibid.

15. History.com Staff, "Dust Bowl."

Chapter 3: CCC Legislation and Administrative Organization

1. Civilian Conservation Corps Legacy, "CCC Brief History," http://www.ccclegacy.org/CCC_Brief_History.html.

2. Wisconsin Historical Society, "Depression and Unemployment: Hard Times in Wisconsin," https://www.wisconsinhistory.org/Records/Article/CS426.

3. Alison T. Otis, William D. Honey, Thomas C. Hogg, and Kimberly K. Lakin, *The Forest Service and the Civilian Conservation Corps: 1933–42* (Washington, DC: United States Department of Agriculture, 1986), chap. 2, https://www.nps.gov/parkhistory/online_books/ccc/ccc/chap2.htm.

4. Paul W. Glad, *The History of Wisconsin: Volume V: War, a New Era, and Depression, 1914–1940* (Madison, WI: State Historical Society of Wisconsin, 1990), 493.

5. Editors of *Encyclopedia Britannica*, "United States Presidential Election of 1932," http://www.britannica.com/EBchecked/topic/1753014/United-States-presidential-election-of-1932.

6. CCC Legacy, "CCC Brief History."

7. Ibid.

8. Ibid.

9. Act of March 31, 1933 (Unemployment Relief Act), Public Law 73–5, 48 STAT 22. National Archives Catalog. https://catalog.archives.gov/id/299830.

10. CCC Legacy, "CCC Brief History."

11. Ibid.

12. Perry H. Merrill, *Roosevelt's Forest Army: A History of the Civilian Conservation Corps, 1933–1942* (Montpelier, VT: Merrill, 1981), 7.

13. Glad, *The History of Wisconsin*, 493.

14. Franklin D. Roosevelt, "Executive Order 6101 Starting the Civilian Conservation Corps," April 5, 1933. Online by Gerhard Peters and John T. Woolley, *The American Presidency Project*, http://www.presidency.ucsb.edu/ws/?pid=14609.

15. Robert Fechner, "Participation of the Department of Labor in the Civilian Conservation Corps," in Civilian Conservation Corps, *Two Years of Emergency Conservation Work (Civilian Conservation Corps): April 5, 1933–March 31, 1935*, based upon reports prepared by Robert Fechner (Washington, DC: Civilian Conservation Corps, 1935), 2–3, https://babel.hathitrust.org/cgi/pt?id=mdp.39015004052794;view=1up;seq=5.

16. R. L. Heinemann, "Civilian Conservation Corps," in *Encyclopedia Virginia*, ed. Brendan Wolfe, https://www.encyclopediavirginia.org/The_Civilian_Conservation_Corps.

17. Civilian Conservation Corps, *Objectives and Results of the Civilian Conservation Corps Program* (Washington, DC: Civilian Conservation Corps, 1938), 7–9.

18. Cody White, "The CCC Indian Division," *Prologue Magazine* 48, no. 2 (2016), https://www.archives.gov/publications/prologue/2016/summer/ccc-id.html.

19. Robert Fechner, "Participation of the Veterans' Administration," in Civilian Conservation Corps, *Two Years of Emergency Conservation Work (Civilian Conservation Corps): April 5, 1933–March 31, 1935*, based upon reports prepared by Robert Fechner (Washington, DC: Civilian Conservation Corps, 1935), 25, https://babel.hathitrust.org/cgi/pt?id=mdp.39015004052794;view=1up;seq=5.

20. Glad, *The History of Wisconsin*, 493.

21. CCC Legacy, "CCC Brief History."

22. Civilian Conservation Corps, *Objectives and Results*, 10.

23. "United States History: Civilian Conservation Corps (CCC)," u-s-history.com, http://www.u-s-history.com/pages/h1586.html.

24. Ibid.

25. Civilian Conservation Corps, *Objectives and Results*, 9.

26. Ray Hoyt, *We Can Take It: A Short Story of the C.C.C.* (New York, NY: American Book Company, 1935), 27–32.

27. United States Department of Agriculture Natural Resource Conservation Service, "More Than 80 Years Helping People Help the Land: A Brief History of NRCS," http://www.nrcs.usda.gov/wps/portal/nrcs/detail/national/about/history/?cid=nrcs143_021392.

28. Otis et al., *The Forest Service*, chap. 8, https://www.nps.gov/parkhistory/online_books/ccc/ccc/chap8.htm.

29. Ibid.

30. Ibid.

31. Ibid.

32. Fechner, *Two Years of Emergency Conservation Work*, 6.

33. Ibid.

34. Merrill, *Roosevelt's Forest Army*, 9.

35. Roy Hoyt, *Your CCC: A Handbook for Enrollees*, 2nd ed. (Washington, DC: Happy Days, 1939), 9.

36. John C. Paige, *The Civilian Conservation Corps and the National Park Service, 1933–1942: An Administrative History* (Washington, DC: National Park Service, United States Department of the Interior, 1985), appendix A, http://www.nps.gov/parkhistory/online_books/ccc/cccaa.htm.

37. Ibid.

38. Hoyt, *Your CCC*, 15.

39. "History, Sparta District, CCC," in *Sparta CCC District, Sixth Corps Area Annual* (Baton Rouge, LA: Direct Advertising Co., 1937), 26, http://www.wisconsinhistory.org/turningpoints/search.asp?id=1651.

40. Ibid., 25–30.

41. Ibid., 25–6.

42. "History, Sparta District, CCC," 26.

43. United States Forest Service, Division of CCC Enrollee Training, *CCC Foremanship* (Washington, DC: United States Forest Service, 1939), 1.

44. "United States Forest Service, Division of CCC Enrollee Training," 2–8.

45. "A Chronicle of Our Past . . . the 1930s," *Triad Online*, http://www.mccoy.army.mil/vtriad_online/90th%20Anniversary%20Triad/chronicle%201930s.htm.

46. Otis et al., *The Forest Service*, chap. 10, http://npshistory.com/publications/usfs/FS-395/chap10.htm.

Chapter 4: The CCC Recruit

1. Jay Scriba, "CCC Fighting the Depression in the Woods," *Milwaukee Journal Sentinel*, September 21, 1970.

2. Personal correspondence from Nancy Williamson, May 12, 2015.

3. Daniel Medina, "Civilian Conservation Corps, Racial Segregation, and the Building of the Angeles National Forest," KCET.org, https://www.kcet.org/shows/departures/civilian-conservation-corps-racial-segregation-and-the-building-of-the-angeles.

4. Ibid.

5. Robert Fechner, "Robert Fechner to Thomas L. Griffith, 21 September 1935," W. W. Norton & Company: Studyspace, http://www.wwnorton.com/college/history/america7_brief/content/multimedia/ch28/research_02e.htm.

6. Digital Public Library of America, "Roosevelt's Tree Army: The Civilian Conservation Corps: Native American Camps," https://dp.la/exhibitions/civilian-conservation-corps/camps-african-american-native/native-american-camps.

7. "The New Deal Agencies: Civilian Conservation Corps," Historical Boys' Clothing, http://histclo.com/essay/war/dep/cou/us/nda-ccc.html.

8. Ray Hoyt, *Your CCC: A Handbook for Enrollees*, 2nd ed. (Washington, DC: Happy Days, 1939), 62.

9. Ibid., 4, 27, 51.

10. Alfred Emile Cornebise, "Heralds in New Deal America: Camp Newspapers of the Civilian Conservation Corps," http://www.scripps.ohiou.edu/mediahistory/mhmjour2–1.htm.

11. Ibid.

12. Ibid.

13. Civilian Conservation Corps Legacy, "CCC Camps Wisconsin," http://www.ccclegacy.org/CCC_Camps_Wisconsin.html.

14. "Newsletter: Nu-Wud-Nus/Camp New Wood, Civilian Conservation Corps," Digital Archives of Broward County Library, http://digitalarchives.broward.org/cdm/ref/collection/ccc/id/2585.

15. *The Voice of 1610*, vol. 1, no. 18, Camp Connors Lake, Phillips, Wisconsin, May 1935.

16. Cornebise, "Heralds in New Deal America."

17. *Camp Irving Weekly*, vol. 4, no. 6, Camp Irving, Black River Falls, Wisconsin, November 6, 1936.

18. *The Civilian Conservation Corp Company 1604 Connection* anniversary booklet, received from Jeanne Evert, February 12, 2015.

19. *The Rusketeer*, vol. 1, no.1, Camp Rusk, Glen Flora, Wisconsin, September 1935.

20. Cornebise, "Heralds in New Deal America."

21. *The Rusketeer*, vol. 1, no. 1.

22. Lawrence E. Kant, "Wood Tick No Discipline U.S. CCC, The Roosevelt Idea." Courtesy of Park Falls Public Library.

23. Hoyt, *Your CCC*, 4.

24. Personal correspondence from Eleanore Schuetz, February 19, 2015.

25. Scott and James Henderson, "Log Cabins a Legacy of Camp Tomahawk," *Northwood River News*, February 23, 2012.

26. Personal correspondence from Paul Waid, January 25, 2015.

27. Personal correspondence from Jeanne Evert, January 25, 2015.

28. Gerald Brock, "Biography of Anthony J. Caffrey," James F. Justin Museum, http://www.justinmuseum.com/oralbio/caffreyajbio.html.

Chapter 5: The Spoolman Journals

1. Personal correspondence from Scott Spoolman, May 15, 2015.

Chapter 6: Wisconsin CCC Camps

1. Town of Washburn, "History of the Town of Washburn," http://townofwashburn.com/index.php/history-of-the-town; Civilian Conservation Corps Legacy, "CCC Camps Wisconsin," http://www.ccclegacy.org/CCC_Camps_Wisconsin.html.

2. CCC Legacy, "CCC Camps Wisconsin."

3. "Badger Camps to be Doubled," *Ironwood Daily Globe*, May 4, 1935.

4. CCC Museum, "Civilian Conservation Corps (1933–1942)," http://rhinelander-resorts.com/ccc.htm.

5. Joyce Laabs, "Civilian Conservation Corps Celebrates Diamond Anniversary," *Lakeland Times*, March 28, 2008.

6. Paul W. Glad, *The History of Wisconsin: Volume V: War, a New Era, and Depression, 1914–1940* (Madison, WI: State Historical Society of Wisconsin, 1990), 494.

7. CCC Legacy, "CCC Camp Lists," http://www.ccclegacy.org/
CCC_Camp_Lists.html.

8. "CCC Camps in Chequamegon National Forest, Wisconsin," James F. Justin
Museum, http://www.justinmuseum.com/famjustin/Wisconsin1.html.

9. "Company 642, Camp Riley Creek (F-3), Fifield, Wisconsin," material
contributed by Maureen Trojak from her personal collection, February 12,
2015.

10. "Life in Riley Creek Camp F-3-W (Wisconsin)," *The Forest Army:
Remembering the Civilian Conservation Corps* (blog), August 1, 2007,
http://forestarmy.blogspot.com/2007/08/life-in-riley-creek-camp-
f-3-w.html.

11. Ibid.

12. "History, Sparta District, CCC," in *Sparta CCC District, Sixth Corps
Area Annual* (Baton Rouge, LA: Direct Advertising Co., 1937), 83–5,
http://www.wisconsinhistory.org/turningpoints/search.asp?id=1651.

13. *The Civilian Conservation Corp Company 1604 Connection* anniversary
booklet, received from Jeanne Evert, February 12, 2015.

14. Personal correspondence from Jeanne Evert, February 12, 2015.

15. Alison T. Otis, William D. Honey, Thomas C. Hogg, and Kimberly K.
Lakin, *The Forest Service and the Civilian Conservation Corps: 1933–42*
(Washington, DC: United States Department of Agriculture, 1986),
chap. 10, http://npshistory.com/publications/usfs/FS-395/
chap10.htm.

16. Kennell M. Elliot, *History of the Nicolet National Forest, 1928–1976*
(Washington, DC: United States Forest Service, 1977), 42–8, https://
foresthistory.org/wp-content/uploads/2017/02/History-of-Nicolet-
National-Forest-1928–1976.pdf.

17. See http://www.rootsweb.ancestry.com/~wioconto/CCC.htm.

18. CCC Legacy, "CCC Brief History," http://www.ccclegacy.org/CCC_Brief_
History.html.

19. Ruth Ann Montgomery, "Evansville Fairgrounds," http://
evansvillehistory.net/fairgrounds.html.

20. Ibid.

21. "History, Sparta District," 114.

Chapter 7: Around a CCC Camp

1. "Life in Riley Creek Camp F-3-W (Wisconsin)," *The Forest Army: Remembering the Civilian Conservation Corps* (blog), August 1, 2007, http://forestarmy.blogspot.com/2007/08/life-in-riley-creek-camp-f-3-w.html.
2. *The Civilian Conservation Corp Company 1604 Connection* anniversary booklet, received from Jeanne Evert, February 12, 2015.
3. "History, Sparta District, CCC," in *Sparta CCC District, Sixth Corps Area Annual* (Baton Rouge, LA: Direct Advertising Co., 1937), 83–5, http://www.wisconsinhistory.org/turningpoints/search.asp?id=1651.
4. Ibid., 36.
5. Personal correspondence from Virginia and Miles Christenson, February 20, 2015.
6. Lawrence E. Kant, "Wood Tick No Discipline U.S. CCC, The Roosevelt Idea," 4. Courtesy of Park Falls Public Library.
7. Guy Christianson, "Biography of Guy Christianson," James F. Justin Museum, http://www.justinmuseum.com/famjustin/Christiansonbio.html.
8. "History, Sparta District, CCC," 190.
9. Ibid., 190–1.

Chapter 8: Everyday Life in a CCC Camp

1. David S. Rouse, "Pages from My Past: The Civilian Conservation Corps," *Wisconsin Magazine of History* 71, no. 3 (1988): 208–9.
2. Rudy Kubiak, "My Experiences in the CCC," in *The Way We Worked* (Eau Claire, WI: Digicopy, 2005), 9–10.
3. Stephanie Daniels, "Locals Look Back on Life in CCC Camps 80 Years Later," *Park Falls Herald*, July 16, 2013.
4. "Conservation Corps Worker Recalls His Camp Riley Days," *The Bee*, September 25, 1980.
5. Ibid.
6. Personal correspondence from Virginia and Miles Christenson, February 20, 2015.
7. Personal correspondence from Scott Spoolman, May 15, 2015.
8. Personal correspondence from Virginia and Miles Christenson.
9. Ray Hoyt, *Your CCC: A Handbook for Enrollees*, 2nd ed. (Washington, DC: Happy Days, 1939), 26.

10. Ray Hoyt, *We Can Take It: A Short Story of the C.C.C.* (New York, NY: American Book Company, 1935), 36.

11. Ibid., 36–7.

12. Personal correspondence from Scott Spoolman.

Chapter 9: Educational, Recreational, and Religious Opportunities

1. Civilian Conservation Corps Legacy, "CCC Brief History," www.ccclegacy .org/CCC_Brief_History.html.

2. Robert J. Moore, *Devil's Lake, Wisconsin and the Civilian Conservation Corps* (Charleston, SC: The History Press, 2011), 44.

3. United States Forest Service, Division of CCC Enrollee Training, *CCC Foremanship* (Washington, DC: United States Forest Service, 1939), 36.

4. Robert Fechner, "Participation of the War Department" in Civilian Conservation Corps, *Two Years of Emergency Conservation Work (Civilian Conservation Corps): April 5, 1933–March 31, 1935*, based upon reports prepared by Robert Fechner (Washington, DC: Civilian Conservation Corps, 1935), 9, https://babel.hathitrust.org/cgi/pt?id=mdp.3901500405 2794;view=1up;seq=5.

5. Perry H. Merrill, *Roosevelt's Forest Army: A History of the Civilian Conservation Corps, 1933–1942* (Montpelier, VT: Merrill, 1981), 66.

6. Moore, *Devil's Lake Wisconsin*, 44.

7. Paul W. Glad, *The History of Wisconsin: Volume V: War, a New Era, and Depression, 1914–1940* (Madison, WI: State Historical Society of Wisconsin, 1990), 494.

8. Alison T. Otis, William D. Honey, Thomas C. Hogg, and Kimberly K. Lakin, *The Forest Service and the Civilian Conservation Corps: 1933–42* (Washington, DC: United States Department of Agriculture, 1986), chap. 10, http://npshistory.com/publications/usfs/FS-395/chap10.htm.

9. Personal correspondence from Lute Berkey, March 14, 2015.

10. Ray Hoyt, *Your CCC: A Handbook for Enrollees*, 2nd ed. (Washington, DC: Happy Days, 1939), 64.

11. Jerry Bayer, "Biography of Jerry Bayer," James F. Justin Museum, http:// www.justinmuseum.com/famjustin/Bayerbio.html.

12. "History, Sparta District, CCC," in *Sparta CCC District, Sixth Corps Area Annual* (Baton Rouge, LA: Direct Advertising Co., 1937), 191–2, http:// www.wisconsinhistory.org/turningpoints/search.asp?id=1651.

13. *The Voice of 1610*, vol. 1, no. 18, Camp Connors Lake, Phillips, Wisconsin, May 1935.

14. US Forest Service, *CCC Foremanship*, 35.

15. Ibid.

16. Ibid, 49–52.

17. *The Voice of 1610*, vol. 1, no. 18.

18. Ray Hoyt, *We Can Take It: A Short Story of the C.C.C.* (New York, NY: American Book Company, 1935), 35.

19. "History, Sparta District, CCC," *Sparta CCC District*, 37, http://www .wisconsinhistory.org/turningpoints/search.asp?id=1651.

20. John Vogel, *Historical Findings: Castle Rock and Petenwell Reservoirs* (La Crosse WI: Mississippi Valley Archaeological Center, 1995), 34–7; "Wisconsin Revisited: Camp Petenwell, the Forgotten CCC Camp," https://wisconsinrevisited.wordpress.com/places/ camp-petenwell-the-forgotten-ccc-camp.

21. Personal correspondence from Virginia and Miles Christenson, February 20, 2015.

22. Moore, *Devil's Lake*, 55.

23. Kathleen Harris, "One Hundred Years of Memories," *Wisconsin Natural Resources* (June 2009), http://dnr.wi.gov/wnrmag/2009/06/park.htm.

24. Hoyt, *Your CCC*, 29.

25. Personal correspondence from Kay Barnard, October 28, 2014.

26. Personal correspondence from Therese Trojak, February 28, 2015.

27. David S. Rouse, "Pages from My Past: The Civilian Conservation Corps," *Wisconsin Magazine of History* 71, no. 3 (1988): 210.

28. Lawrence E. Kant, "Wood Tick No Discipline U.S. CCC, The Roosevelt Idea." Courtesy of Park Falls Public Library.

Chapter 10: Community Relations

1. David S. Rouse, "Pages from My Past: the Civilian Conservation Corps," *Wisconsin Magazine of History* 71, no. 3 (1988): 214.

2. "School Band Entertained at Sheep Ranch Camp," *Phillipsonian*, December, 1935.

3. Emery Centennial Committee, "Civilian Conservation Corps & N.R.A.," in *Town of Emery Centennial 1889–1989* (Park Falls, WI: F. A. Weber & Sons, 1989), 14–17.

4. "Great Dance Stirs Peaceful Quiet of Lonely Riverside," http://
   riblakehistory.com/Rib%20Lake%20History%2011800–11899/11810A-
   history%20of%20CCC%20Camp%20Mondeaux%201933–1937.pdf.

5. Guy Christianson, "Biography of Guy Christianson," James F. Justin
   Museum, http://www.justinmuseum.com/famjustin/Christiansonbio
   .html.

6. Quoted in Joyce Laabs, "Civilian Conservation Corps Celebrates Diamond
   Anniversary," *Lakeland Times*, March 28, 2008.

7. Interview with James Skarda, May 6, 2015.

8. Robert J. Moore, *Devil's Lake, Wisconsin and the Civilian Conservation Corps*
   (Charleston, SC: The History Press, 2011), 62.

9. "Mother Is Rescued by CCC Enrollees," *Ironwood Daily Globe*, January 26,
   1938.

10. Laabs, "Civilian Conservation Corps Celebrates Diamond Anniversary."

Chapter 11: Overview of Projects

1. Robert Fechner, "Report on the Operations of Emergency Conservation
   Work (Civilian Conservation Corps)" in Civilian Conservation Corps, *Two
   Years of Emergency Conservation Work (Civilian Conservation Corps): April
   5, 1933–March 31, 1935*, based upon reports prepared by Robert Fechner
   (Washington, DC: Civilian Conservation Corps, 1935), 8, https://babel
   .hathitrust.org/cgi/pt?id=mdp.39015004052794;view=1up;seq=5.

2. Perry H. Merrill, *Roosevelt's Forest Army: A History of the Civilian Conservation Corps, 1933–1942* (Montpelier, VT: Merrill, 1981), 9.

3. See http://www.treesfortomorrow.com/index.php/ccc-tft-ties? for more
   information on Trees for Tomorrow.

4. Civilian Conservation Corps, *Objectives and Results of the Civilian
   Conservation Corps Program* (Washington, DC: Civilian Conservation
   Corps, 1938), 12.

5. Ray Hoyt, *Your CCC: A Handbook for Enrollees*, 2nd ed. (Washington, DC:
   Happy Days, 1939), 14–15.

6. David S. Rouse, "Pages from My Past: The Civilian Conservation Corps,"
   Wisconsin Magazine of History 71, no. 3 (1988): 212–13.

7. "History, Sparta District, CCC," in *Sparta CCC District, Sixth Corps Area
   Annual* (Baton Rouge, LA: Direct Advertising Co., 1937), 24, http://www
   .wisconsinhistory.org/turningpoints/search.asp?id=1651.

Chapter 12: Forestry and Fish Hatchery Work

1. "History, Sparta District, CCC," in *Sparta CCC District, Sixth Corps Area Annual* (Baton Rouge, LA: Direct Advertising Co., 1937), 179, http://www.wisconsinhistory.org/turningpoints/search.asp?id=1651.

2. Alison T. Otis, William D. Honey, Thomas C. Hogg, and Kimberly K. Lakin, *The Forest Service and the Civilian Conservation Corps: 1933–42* (Washington, DC: United States Department of Agriculture, 1986), chap. 10, http://npshistory.com/publications/usfs/FS-395/chap10.htm.

3. Alan G. Barbian, "Strong Shoulders of the CCC in the National Forest," *Park Falls Herald*, July 14, 2005.

4. "Franklin Lake Campground-Eagle River, WI," The Living New Deal, https://livingnewdeal.org/projects/franklin-lake-campground-eagle-river-wi.

5. Lawrence E. Kant, "Wood Tick No Discipline U.S. CCC, The Roosevelt Idea," 26. Courtesy of Park Falls Public Library.

6. Personal correspondence from Scott Spoolman, May 15, 2015.

7. "CCC Camp Mondeaux River, Company 1603, Camp No. F-18," http://riblakehistory.com/Rib%20Lake%20History%2011800–11899/11810A-history%20of%20CCC%20Camp%20Mondeaux%201933–1937.pdf.

8. Quoted in Joyce Laabs, "Civilian Conservation Corps Celebrates Diamond Anniversary," *Lakeland Times*, March 28, 2008.

9. Thunder River Fish Rearing Station (property record for W13562 Hatchery Rd. [Marinette County], architecture and history inventory), Wisconsin Historical Society, https://www.wisconsinhistory.org/Records/Property/HI22663.

10. Arthur A. Oehmcke, *The Woodruff Hatchery Story* (Wisconsin: A. A. Oehmcke, 1989), 21.

11. Lisa Gaumnitz, "Taking Stock of State Hatcheries," *Wisconsin Natural Resources* (February 2003), http://dnr.wi.gov/wnrmag/html/stories/2003/feb03/hatch.htm.

Chapter 13: Soil and Water Conservation Work

1. Renae Anderson and Barbara Jansen, *Wisconsin Conservation History* (Madison, WI: United States Department of Agriculture, Natural Resources Conservation Service, 2010), 8.

2. Personal correspondence from Sister Carmen Mulcahy, Ph.D., June 2015.

3. Leonard C. Johnson, *Soil Conservation in Wisconsin: Birth to Rebirth* (Madison, WI: Department of Soil Science, University of Wisconsin, 1961), 37.

4. Ibid., 41.

5. Anderson and Jansen, *Wisconsin Conservation History*, 15.

6. Ibid., 8.

7. Soil Science Society of America, "Aldo Leopold and the Coon Valley Watershed Conservation Project," https://www.soils.org/discover-soils/story/aldo-leopold-and-coon-valley-watershed-conservation-project.

8. Interview with Clarence Olson, February 11, 2015.

9. University of Wisconsin Department of Agronomy, *University of Wisconsin Agronomy Department: The First 100 Years* (Madison, WI: University of Wisconsin Department of Agronomy, 2003), 83–4.

10. Jennifer Wieman, "Vernon County's Oldest Soil-Save Dam Repaired after Sustaining Flood Damage," *Vernon Broadcaster*, October 27, 2011.

11. Ansel Burton Bratberg, *Long Ago, Long Coulee* (Onalaska, WI: Miller Quick Print, 2012), 38–41.

12. Robert J. Moore, "Louis Roedell and the CCC," *Mt. Horeb Area Past Times* (July 2014): 1–5, 8.

13. "History, Sparta District, CCC," in *Sparta CCC District, Sixth Corps Area Annual* (Baton Rouge, LA: Direct Advertising Co., 1937), 128–130, http://www.wisconsinhistory.org/turningpoints/search.asp?id=1651.

14. Interviews with James Skarda, May 6, 2015, and May 18, 2015.

15. Interview with James Skarda, May 18, 2015.

16. Interviews with James Skarda, May 6, 2015, and May 18, 2015.

17. Interview with Jimmy Bramblett, September 2, 2015.

Chapter 14: State Park, County Park, and Municipal Projects

1. Carol Ahlgren, "The Civilian Conservation Corps and Wisconsin State Park Development," *Wisconsin Magazine of History* 71, no. 3 (1988): 186–8.

2. Ibid., 196.

3. Cynthia M. Stiles, "The Fruits of Their Labor," *Wisconsin Natural Resources* (October 1992): 5.

4. National Geodetic Survey, "The NGS Data Sheet," https://www.ngs.noaa.gov/cgi-bin/ds_mark.prl?PidBox=QN0476.

5. "Rib Mountain State Park: History," Wisconsin Department of Natural Resources, http://dnr.wi.gov/topic/parks/name/ribmt/history.html.

6. "Copper Falls State Park: History," Wisconsin Department of Natural Resources, http://dnr.wi.gov/topic/parks/name/copperfalls/history .html.

7. Interview with Kent Goeckerman, February 11, 2015.

8. Ibid.

9. Ibid.

10. Ibid.

11. "Men Left Historic Mark on State Park," *Milwaukee Journal Sentinel*, October 30, 2005.

12. "Perrot State Park: History," Wisconsin Department of Natural Resources, http://dnr.wi.gov/topic/parks/name/perrot/history.html.

13. "Pattison State Park: History," Wisconsin Department of Natural Resources, http://dnr.wi.gov/topic/parks/name/pattison/history.html.

14. "Peninsula State Park: History," Wisconsin Department of Natural Resources, http://dnr.wi.gov/topic/parks/name/peninsula/history.html.

15. William H. Tishler, *Door County's Emerald Treasure: A History of Peninsula State Park* (Madison, WI: University of Wisconsin Press, 2006), 159.

16. Ibid., 160.

17. Ibid. 168–9.

18. Kathleen Harris, "One Hundred Years of Memories," *Wisconsin Natural Resources* (June 2009), http://dnr.wi.gov/wnrmag/2009/06/park.htm.

19. "Wyalusing State Park–Bagley, WI," The Living New Deal, http://living newdeal.org/projects/wyalusing-state-park-bagley-wi; "Wyalusing State Park: History," Wisconsin Department of Natural Resources, http://dnr .wi.gov/topic/parks/name/wyalusing/history.html.

20. "Devil's Lake State Park: 100 Years of Stories," Wisconsin Department of Natural Resources, http://dnr.wi.gov/topic/parks/name/devilslake/ history.html.

21. Robert J. Moore, *Devil's Lake, Wisconsin and the Civilian Conservation Corps* (Charleston, SC: The History Press, 2011), 33.

22. David S. Rouse, "Pages from My Past: The Civilian Conservation Corps," *Wisconsin Magazine of History* 71, no. 3 (1988): 206.

23. Moore, *Devil's Lake*, 86–7.

24. United States Department of the Interior, National Park Service, National Register of Historic Places Registration Form, Dells of the Eau Claire County Park, Town of Plover, Marathon County, Wisconsin (December 19, 2014, Section 8), 8–9, 16.

25. Lois M. Quinn, John Pawasarat, and Laura Serebin, *Jobs for Workers on Relief in Milwaukee County, 1930–1994* (Milwaukee, WI: University of Wisconsin, Milwaukee, 1995), 38, https://www4.uwm.edu/eti/reprints/JobsCCCNYA.pdf.

26. See https://milwaukeehistory.net for CCC work in Milwaukee.

27. "Estabrook Park–Milwaukee, WI," The Living New Deal, https://living newdeal.org/projects/estabrook-park-milwaukee-wi.

28. "A Brief History of Kletzsch Park," https://www.kletzschfriends.org/kletzsch-park-history.

29. "Milwaukee County Landmarks: Cudahy," https://milwaukeehistory.net/education/county-landmarks/cudahy/.

30. "History and Tour of Boerner Botanical Gardens," http://county.milwaukee.gov/Tour10499.htm?docid=10499 and http://county.milwaukee.gov/ConstructionampHisto10500.htm?docid=10500.

Chapter 15: The University of Wisconsin Arboretum

1. University of Wisconsin Arboretum, "History," https://arboretum.wisc.edu/about-us/history/.

2. Thomas J. Blewett and Grant Cottam, "History of the University of Wisconsin Arboretum Prairies," *Transactions of the Wisconsin Academy of Sciences, Arts and Letters* 72, (1984): 130.

3. University of Wisconsin Arboretum, "History."

4. Franklin E. Court, *Pioneers of Ecological Restoration: The People and Legacy of the University of Wisconsin Arboretum* (Madison, WI: University of Wisconsin Press, 2012), 83.

5. Ibid., 86.

6. Ibid., 87.

7. Ibid., 94.

8. Ibid., 92.

9. Interview with Molly Fifield Murray, June 2, 2015.

10. Ibid.

11. Court, *Pioneers of Ecological Restoration*, 100.

12. Blewett and Cottam, "History of the University of Wisconsin Arboretum Prairies," 131. See also Court, *Pioneers of Ecological Restoration*, 92–3.

13. Blewett and Cottam, "History of the University of Wisconsin Arboretum Prairies," 132.

14. Interview with Molly Fifield Murray.

15. Levi Wood, "The CCC and the Arboretum," University of Wisconsin Arboretum, https://arboretum.wisc.edu/news/naturalists-notes/the-ccc-and-the-arboretum-2/.

16. Interview with Molly Fifield Murray.

Chapter 16: CCC and Its Critics

1. John A. Salmond, *The Civilian Conservation Corps, 1933–1942: A New Deal Case Study* (Durham, NC: Duke University Press, 1967), chap. 1, http://www.nps.gov/parkhistory/online_books/ccc/salmond/chap1.htm.

2. Carol Ahlgren, "The Civilian Conservation Corps and Wisconsin State Park Development," *Wisconsin Magazine of History* 71, no. 3 (1988): 190.

3. Paul W. Glad, *The History of Wisconsin: Volume V: War, a New Era, and Depression, 1914–1940* (Madison, WI: State Historical Society of Wisconsin, 1990), 495.

4. Ibid.

5. John A. Garraty, *The Great Depression* (Garden City, NY: Anchor Books, 1987), 182.

6. Ibid., 185.

7. Ibid., 189.

8. Aldo Leopold, "Conservation Economics," *Journal of Forestry* XXXII, no. 5 (1934): 540.

9. Glad, *The History of Wisconsin*, 496.

10. Personal correspondence from Curt Meine, February 12, 2015.

11. USDA Forest Service, *The USDA Forest Service—The First Century* (Washington, DC: USDA Forest Service Office of Communication, 2005), 68, https://www.fs.fed.us/sites/default/files/media/2015/06/The_USDA_Forest_Service_TheFirstCentury.pdf.

12. Glad, *The History of Wisconsin*, 498.

13. Salmond, *The Civilian Conservation Corps*, chap. 6, http://www.nps.gov/parkhistory/online_books/ccc/salmond/chap6.htm.

Chapter 17: Accomplishments and Accolades

1. Civilian Conservation Corps, *Objectives and Results of the Civilian Conservation Corps Program* (Washington, DC: Civilian Conservation Corps, 1938), 2.

2. Jerry Bayer, "Biography of Jerry Bayer," James F. Justin Museum, http://www.justinmuseum.com/famjustin/Bayerbio.html.

3. David S. Rouse, "Pages from My Past: The Civilian Conservation Corps," *Wisconsin Magazine of History* 71, no. 3 (1988): 216.

4. Interview with James Skarda, May 6, 2015.

5. Email correspondence from Joan Palmer, January 6, 2015.

6. Personal correspondence from Kay Scholtz, January 24, 2015.

7. Interview with Kent Goeckerman, February 11, 2015.

8. Colin Taylor Higgins, "From Forest to Field: Nature, the State, and the New Deal in Rural Wisconsin," *The Indiana University Undergraduate Journal of History* 4, no. 1 (2013): 26–8.

9. Ibid.

10. Neil M. Maher, *Nature's New Deal* (New York, NY: Oxford University Press, 2008), 155.

11. Ibid.

12. Ibid., 158.

13. Civilian Conservation Corps, *Objectives and Results*, 35.

14. Sally Ann Gumaer Ranney, "Women and the History of American Conservation," *Women in Natural Resources* 11, no. 3 (March 1990): 44–50.

15. Emery Centennial Committee, "Civilian Conservation Corps & N.R.A.," in *Town of Emery Centennial 1889–1989* (Park Falls, WI: F. A. Weber & Sons, 1989), 14–17.

Chapter 18: The Program Ends

1. David E. Conrad, Jay H. Cravens, and the US Forest Service, *The Land We Cared For: A History of the Forest Service's Eastern Region* (Carbondale, IL: American Resources Group, 1997), 106.

2. Ibid.

3. Ibid.

4. "Forests survive W.W. II," *Daily Press*, November 5, 2005.

5. Carol Ahlgren, "The Civilian Conservation Corps and Wisconsin State Park Development," *Wisconsin Magazine of History* 71, no. 3 (1988): 204.

Chapter 19: Memories Remain

1. Civilian Conservation Corps Legacy, "CCC Statue List," http://www
   .ccclegacy.org/CCC_Statue_List.html.
2. "CCC Worker Statute Dedication June 14," *Lakeland Times*, June 5, 2015.
3. Interview with Cheryl Westbrook, July 25, 2015.
4. Interview with Aprelle Rowski, July 25, 2015.
5. CCC Legacy, http://www.ccclegacy.org.
6. Written by an anonymous CCC alumnus and read at the CCC Alumni
   Waupaca Area Chapter 54 annual Christmas banquet, December 3, 1985,
   by Harland Hansen, who was assigned to Camp Tomahawk in CCC Company 1608. Material from Marilyn Hansen Apps.

Acknowledgments

As with all of my books, many people helped every step of the way. I first want to thank Jane Janke. It was Jane who suggested I write a book about the CCC. After I put out the word that I was looking for CCC stories and photos, I was pleasantly surprised by the response. The following people sent me invaluable materials—stories, letters, journals, photos, and other CCC memorabilia—and often leads as to where to find additional materials. A huge thank you to each: Tim Montgomery, Paul Waid, Jeanne Evert, Scott Spoolman, Virginia and Miles Christenson, Bill and Helen Campbell, Clarita Wenzel, Lute Berkey, Kay Barnard, Therese Trojak, Rick Bernstein, Maureen Trojak, Jeff Bock, Sister Carmen Mulcahy, Clarence Olson, Joan Palmer, Kay Schultz, Marilyn Hansen Apps, Natasha Kassulke, Curt Meine, Jean Meyer, Eleanore Schuetz, Greg Smith, John Werth, Grady Gutknecht, Michael Smith, Karen Dums, Nancy Williamson, Howard Sherpe, Joan Sanstadt, Doug Goetz, Karl Lambon, Pat Leavenworth, Dennis Dadacki, Rachelle Towne, Sheri Zillmer, Pete Morgan, Ricki Bishop, Andy Burkart, John Duchac, Gary Knowles, John Bauer, Mary Farrell Stieve, Ed Spitzbarth, Matt Waid, Michael Yanny, Mary Schueller, Mary Jane Herber, K. S. Pittsley, Laura Middleton, Mary Erickson, William Duncanson, Leah Rhodes, Gerald Glaeve, Kelly J. Herold, Steve Sylvester, Dennis Nash, Victoria Goff, Kristi Williams, Michael Smith, Jane Barany, and Susan Apps-Bodilly.

Thank you to those I interviewed for this project: James Skarda, in his nineties and once a CCC enrollee at Camp Viroqua; Kent Goeckerman, former superintendent of Copper Falls State Park; Cheryl Westbrook, Rhinelander CCC Museum; Aprelle Rowski, museum coordinator, Pioneer Park, Rhinelander; Molly Fifield Murray, former outreach programs manager, University of Wisconsin–Madison Arboretum; and Jimmy Bramblett, former state conservationist, the USDA Natural Resources Conservation Service.

A special thanks to my son Steve Apps, who took several photos for the book. And to my wife, Ruth, a huge thank you. She has tirelessly, for more than fifty years, read all of my writing and is never hesitant to give it a thumbs up or a thumbs down. Another huge thank you to Tom Krause, editor at the Wisconsin Historical Society Press, who had the onerous task of figuring out what I was trying to say in this book and then helping me say it. I appreciate his attention to detail, especially those details that I had wrong.

And lastly, thank you to Kate Thompson, director of the Wisconsin Historical Society Press, who has long supported my writing and who encouraged me every step of the way on this project.

Index

Page numbers in *italic* refer to illustrations.

About the Author

Jerry Apps has written more than thirty-five books on rural history and environmental issues. He is a former county extension agent and professor for the University of Wisconsin College of Agricultural and Life Sciences. In 2012, he was elected a Fellow in the Wisconsin Academy of Sciences, Arts and Letters.